Teaching Music to the Exceptional Child

A Handbook for Mainstreaming

Richard M. Graham
University of Georgia

Alice S. Beer
Baltimore City Public Schools

Prentice-Hall, Inc., Englewood Cliffs, N.J. 07632

Library of Congress Cataloging in Publication Data

GRAHAM, RICHARD M.
  Teaching music to the exceptional child.

  Bibliography: p. 189
  Includes index.
  1. Handicapped children—Education—Music.
2. Exceptional children—Education—Music. 3. School
music—Instruction and study. I. Beer, Alice S., joint
author. I. Title.
MT1.G78   371.9'044   79–19322
ISBN   0–13–893982–9
ISBN   0–13–893974–8 pbk.

Printed in the United States of America

10   9   8   7   6   5   4   3   2   1

Editorial/production supervision by Douglas Kubach
Interior design by Cindy Marione
Cover design by Saiki/Sprung Design
Manufacturing buyer: Ed Leone

Prentice-Hall International, Inc., *London*
Prentice-Hall of Australia Pty. Limited, *Sydney*
Prentice-Hall of Canada, Ltd., *Toronto*
Prentice-Hall of India Private Limited, *New Delhi*
Prentice-Hall of Japan, Inc., *Tokyo*
Prentice-Hall of Southeast Asia Pte. Ltd., *Singapore*
Whitehall Books Limited, *Wellington, New Zealand*

Contents

6. Moving,   159

Preface

The purpose of this book is to offer a basis for preservice and inservice training in music education of handicapped children. The book is written so as to be in accord with the fundamental tenets of the Education for All Handicapped Children Act of 1975 (Public Law 94-142) and other group and individual movements which are positively related to that precedent-setting legislation.

Specifically, this book is designed to bring about learning experiences for teachers, teacher trainees, school administrators, parents, therapists, counselors, and others in the following four areas:

1. Planning and writing of music education goals and objectives into the child's individualized educational program (IEP)
2. Preparation of "regular" school personnel to deal with handicapped children in school music learning situations
3. Developing skills for the music teacher of handicapped children in the least restrictive environment commensurate with their needs or "mainstreaming" in music education
4. Assessment of handicapped children and their music education programs in order that both might be modified in favor of the child's growth and development, musical and otherwise

The music education model employed in this book is based upon the normal pattern of musical development through which every child grows.

The model reflects patterns of development that begin with a chronology of emerging musical abilities in the preschool child in two principal areas: (1) singing abilities, and (2) manipulative and movement abilities. The activities presented in the book reflect the sequence of musical behaviors as they stem from the preschool child's singing and manipulative–movement abilities through the full development of these behaviors as legitimate means of musical expression recognized and valued in American culture. These developmental experiences lead to competencies in the following:

1. Singing
2. Playing musical instruments
3. Listening to music
4. Creating music
5. Moving expressively to music

The development of music-reading skills is shown in the model as relating to and growing from interest and accumulating competencies in any one or a combination of the above five areas.

In outlining musical development through developmentally oriented music activities, the authors have made available a plan for assistance to those who plan, teach, and assess the musical growth of handicapped and normal children from preschool through young adulthood. Though these activities have been designed so that they can be taught by any musical regular teacher, the teaching would probably be done most effectively by a music specialist working full time or, if that is not possible, in some form of support capacity with a regular teacher. (In this book the term *music specialist* refers to a certified music educator, music therapist, or regular classroom teacher with recognized music teaching credentials.)

Where mainstreaming occurs in performing ensembles—usually in secondary grade levels—the music specialist would normally be available. In the far greater number of instances in the lower grades, it will be the regular classroom teacher who has the responsibility to teach music to classes that include handicapped children. In situations where new alliances are being developed among classroom teacher, special educator, and music educator, the need for a methodology common to the three specialists becomes evident. A new interdisciplinary methodology would combine relevant techniques from music education and special education to be presented within the context of the regular teacher's plan of work. In selecting activities to be presented in this work, the authors were ever mindful of the need to include music learning experiences which would be conducive to multidisciplinary efforts in planning, teaching, and assessment. It will be seen that most of the music activities can be used to meet esthetic and practical needs of handicapped and nonhandicapped children in the same classroom setting. The activities are designed to meet special education and music education goals, a fact that should greatly facilitate any interdisciplinary planning which involves music experiences.

Teaching Music to the Exceptional Child differs from other music education methods books. The reason for this difference is that the problem being addressed is clearly a new one which calls for new solutions. In order to develop individualized educational programs (IEP) in music for any class that includes exceptional children, the teacher and others involved will be required to think and plan from new perspectives. Much of the experience gained from teaching music in "special rooms" or in training schools will be of little value in planning and teaching music in a class where children exhibit many levels of music ability and interest. This book is designed to facilitate thinking and planning appropriate to contemporary problems related to mainstreaming. Accordingly, the following points are emphasized:

1. There is some aspect of music which can be enjoyed and learned by any child who shows any evidence of capacity to learn, regardless of the severity of a handicapping condition.

2. Since music should not be taught apart from the child's total individualized educational program, the activities suggested here are designed with special education as well as music education objectives in mind.

3. Considerable attention is paid to procedures for esthetic education and development of the child regardless of his or her rate of development or style of learning.

4. For each model activity presented, the reason for its presentation is explained for purposes of planning and assessment.

5. Maximum emphasis is placed upon music making by the child to facilitate learning in the least restrictive environment.

6. Emphasis is placed upon the interdisciplinary team relationship among music educator, regular classroom teacher, and special educator.

The preparation of this book and particularly the music education model has involved many people. A large number of them were associated with the Music and Special Education Departments of the Baltimore City Public Schools. Expressions of gratitude are due to Cheelan Bo-Linn, Waetina Coles, Jean Dunlap, Jack Engeman, Thomas Foster, George Gonderman, Charlotte Hayes, Bruce Horner, Annette Houston,

William Jenkins, Martha McCoy, Prentis Nolan, Michael Rohrbacher, and Joanne Warres. The cooperation and support of these school administrators, principals, music therapists, and music teachers were cherished and deeply appreciated.

I

MUSIC EDUCATION AND THE EXCEPTIONAL CHILD

1 *Music Education and Mainstreaming*

INTRODUCTION

The trend in American education toward the integration of handicapped children into regular classes, including music classes, became notable throughout the country shortly after 1970. The appearance, for the first time in the history of most schools, of handicapped children in bands, orchestras, choruses, and elementary music classes was a reflection of changing attitudes toward education of the handicapped throughout the nation. It would be difficult to point out precisely where and how this movement started. It would not be difficult, however, to enumerate many of the individuals, groups, and events that have given impetus to the movement toward equal education for the handicapped; this has been well documented elsewhere. One of the high points of the movement toward equal education for the handicapped was reached with the passage by the Congress of the United States of the Education for All Handicapped Children Act of 1975, Public Law 94-142. This and other legislation, action by courts, and pressure from interest groups and professional organizations has brought about the initiation of programs to integrate handicapped children with nonhandicapped children for education in regular classrooms. *Mainstreaming* is the term used to describe the practice which, according to its proponents, is to become the rule for educating handicapped children in the future. The chronology of events leading up to mainstreaming and related changes in American educational practice has been listed elsewhere with background information on P.L. 94-142 (Gearheart and Weishahn, 1976; Reynolds and Birch, 1977; *The Unfinished Revolution*, 1976). Every educator would do well to acquaint himself with the chronology of events leading up to the events of the 1970s. For music educators there promise to be fundamental and widespread changes in the established practices of the past.

Mainstreaming has already had considerable impact on many music education programs around the country. The practice will undoubtedly continue to influence the direction of the profession for many years to come. In response to these influences many states are requiring music educators who are to be certified sometime between 1978 and 1980 and from that point afterward to have some college preparation in the education of handicapped children. Some states are providing inservice training for music educators who are presently teaching but who have had no prior education or experience in the area of education of the handicapped. Several states and local school agencies have organized curriculum committees made up of music educators, special educators, and others for the purpose of preparing curriculum guides for music education of the handicapped in mainstreaming situations.

These developments in music education and in other areas of American education reflect a singular and increasingly persistent point of view: that handicapped children shall be more included in the mainstream of American academic and social life. Music educators and other art educators would logically pick up the theme by adding that these children shall also be included in the mainstream of American artistic and cultural life. To the music educator the message portends the inevitable demise of "limited" musical experiences in "special" classrooms or institutions for most handicapped children. It strongly suggests that music education must be made available to all children, including exceptional children at their individual levels of musical capability, and that this must be done in the regular classroom or music room.

Mainstreaming does not mean the simple dumping of handicapped children into certain classes such as music, physical education, and art while "tracking" or "grouping" practices are maintained in academic classes. Unfortunately, some instances of such practice have been reported, and when the music class is the recipient of such dumping, an impossible situation is created. Generally speaking, mainstreaming is based upon an attitude of inclusion for the good of all children in a regular class environment. This attitude must exist throughout the school and be reflected in the total scheduling and planning of the school. The music educator must be prepared to deal with mainstreaming but should feel assured that students, teachers, and administrators alike are totally involved in the process throughout the entire school. It should be added at this point that even the most ardent supporters of mainstreaming realize and support the fact that in some cases—but far fewer than were previously thought to exist—children should be referred to special rooms or even to institutions for the best individualized instruction. Even when such is the case, it is worth restating that the primary effort of mainstreaming remains one of developing and supporting regular classroom settings in such a manner that exceptional children can be served effectively there, along with their nonexceptional classmates.

Mainstreaming in music classes should be supported by music specialists if such classes are not taught entirely by them. When a regular classroom teacher has the responsibility of teaching music to classes which include handicapped children, that teacher should receive support from the administration of the school in the form of scheduling, facilities, and equipment. Whenever available, a music specialist should be made available in a support or advisory role. In addition, support for mainstreaming in music education includes coordination of efforts of regular teacher, music specialist, and school administrator in writing music goals and objectives into the students' individualized educational programs (IEPs). With such a cooperative approach to music teaching, in which singing, playing musical instruments, listening, creating music, and moving bodily to music are all offered on an individualized basis and supported by the school administration, success of the program in terms of musical growth of all children involved will be much more likely. One criterion for success of mainstreaming in music education is that as few handicapped children as possible are forced from integrated music classes back into isolated music experiences of former times. To meet the requirements of the future, music educators and others who teach music to classes that include handicapped children should think and plan in terms of the 1976 definition for mainstreaming published by the Council for Exceptional Children. It covers practically every aspect of mainstreaming:

> Mainstreaming is a belief which involves an educational placement procedure and process for exceptional children, based on the conviction that each such child should be educated in the least restrictive environment in which his educational and related needs can be satisfactorily provided. This concept recognizes that exceptional children have a wide range of special educational needs, varying greatly in intensity and duration; that there is a recognized continuum of educational settings which may, at a given time, be appropriate; that exceptional children should be educated with nonexceptional children; and that special classes, separate schooling, or other removal of an exceptional child from education with nonexceptional children should occur only when the intensity of the child's special education and related needs is such that they cannot be satisfied in an environment including nonexceptional children, even with the provision of supplementary aids and services ["Official Actions . . . Council for Exceptional Children," 1976, p. 43].

A HISTORICAL PERSPECTIVE OF MUSIC EDUCATION OF THE HANDICAPPED IN THE UNITED STATES

The history of music education of the handicapped in the United States can be divided into the following three major eras:

1. Music training in the institutions for the handicapped in the nineteenth century
2. Music experiences in the public school special rooms from 1900 to the late 1960s
3. The beginnings of individualized methodologies from the 1960s to the present

There is considerable overlap of these time periods and it would be inaccurate to assume definite dividing points between the practices indicated above. The time designations presented reflect general trends, and this fact should be kept in mind during any discussion of the history of music education of the handicapped.

THE COLONIAL PERIOD: THE BEGINNINGS OF METHOD

From the mid-eighteenth century through the period of the Revolutionary War, very little of the struggling new nation's energies could be spared for the education of its children. The handicapped in the colonies were ignored as they were throughout the remainder of the world. Music instruction was made available for the talented few of those wealthy enough to afford such a luxury. The movement to group instruction in music and the motivation for such a movement stemmed from the need to improve congregational singing in the churches of the time. This need was felt throughout all the colonies, and in a brief span of some twenty years dating from 1720, singing schools appeared (Birge, 1937). The method of teaching singing was described in a dispatch from Moses Cheney (born in 1776):

> The sessions were held either in the homes of the members or in the school house. At the first meeting boards were placed on kitchen chairs to answer for seats and all the candidates for membership paraded around the room in a circle, the singing master in the center. The master then read the rules, instructing all to pay attention to the rising and falling of the notes. Books containing individual parts, treble, counter, tenor and

bass were distributed, and directions for pitch were given. Then the master commenced. "Now follow me right up and down; sound." So the master sounded and the pupils sounded and in this way some learned to sing by note and others by imitation.

The singing schools began for religious reasons, but the system for teaching which grew from them was incorporated into the social life from one generation to the next until it became one of the accepted institutions of the common people. By the beginning of the nineteenth century, singing school methodology was so well known throughout the country that teaching of any form of choral music and music reading took this as accepted procedure. The techniques of the singing school provided the first music-teaching methods used to train handicapped children in the institutions of the nineteenth century.

MUSIC IN THE INSTITUTIONS
OF THE NINETEENTH CENTURY

The nineteenth century saw the development of institutions for the handicapped throughout the world. In the United States the motivations for institutionalization were varied, but there was never any question of the need for religious services on a regular basis. As had been the case in colonial churches, the need to improve the quality of these religious services led to singing instruction for the handicapped inmates. There are indications that such well-known personages as Julia Ward Howe provided singing instructions for the blind and retarded inmates of the Perkins Institution of Boston at the middle part of the century.

The marching-and-singing technique from the singing school was incorporated in toto into the institutions. Doren (1878) describes the technique still in practice at the State Institution at Columbus as late as 1878:

> The children at the institution assembled four mornings a week for singing and marching exercises. We have been much surprised at the results from the musical training of our children. We have known that many of them possessed musical ability, but have never felt that as an institution we could undertake their training. We overcame all those scruples in January of the present year 1878 and organized an orchestra. The band [sic] consists of two cornets, a bass horn, bass viol, violincello [sic], two first violins, three second, one flageolet, one flute, triangle, etc. It is very curious indeed that some of these children, who can scarcely read, stand up and read their music and play in perfect time [p. 104].

The statement above indicates that music education was an effort taken very seriously by the entire institution. Some of the music programs in institutions developed performing ensembles of a high level, a cause for considerable pride for those associated with the effort. Note the following by Wilbur (1876) regarding his singing classes at the Illinois Asylum for Feebleminded Children:

> One hour of the forenoon is spent with those who seem to have a taste for vocal music in teaching them to sing. The singing of the pupils of this special music class will compare with that of any school in the land [p. 240].

The music groups in institutions eventually came to be known for their performance prowess and in many cases held regular concerts for their fellow inmates and for visitors. Institutional records from several eastern states show records of frequency of musical performance that are highly suggestive of exploitation of the performing inmates. Toward the end of the nineteenth century it was common practice in some institutions to have bands perform at horse shows, regional fairs, carnivals, and picnics. Singing groups were also frequently on display for a variety of clearly noneducational purposes.

Music programs were a common and vital part of the activity programs in all institutions for the handicapped toward the end of the nineteenth century and well into the twentieth. The handicapped individuals who participated in these ongoing musical programs were selected on the basis of interest and talent and in most cases were taught to perform. Some institutional inmates spent most of their lifetime "assigned to the band." There are many reports of how well these children performed but practically no mention of whether or not they enjoyed the experience. In this sense, the institutional music programs of the time were not greatly different from those in the public schools. Music education for institutionalized handicapped and public school child alike was a matter of drill and recitation. There is some evidence that in some instances the institutional music product might have surpassed that of the schools.

As the nineteenth century came to an end, institutional music programs continued to grow; they would continue to do so in one form or another for the next fifty or sixty years. With the development of the profession of psychiatry and continued emphasis on "cure" of the handicapped, many music programs came to be justified in terms of their curative or corrective possibilities. The exploitive practices continued but with accompanying claims of how much "better" the handicapped individual would become as a result of his participation in the band or singing group. With the development of special classes in the public schools, music programs continued to be justified in terms of how certain music activities would benefit the child by ameliorating his or her handicapping condition.

MUSIC IN THE PUBLIC SCHOOL SPECIAL
ROOMS: 1900 TO THE LATE 1960s

Shortly before the turn of the century, educational programs for the handicapped were being developed in a number of cities. Steinbach (1904) reported formation of the first special class in the public schools of Cleveland as early as 1875. Most of the programs before 1900 were not successful mainly because they were planned to bring the handicapped to the level of "normalcy" of nonhandicapped in regular classes. Music was an accepted part of the special class curriculum from the beginning. The music training methods were essentially the same as those employed in the institutional music programs of the time. This is understandable in that the teachers for special classes were recruited directly from the institutions. In a report on newly organized special classes in Cleveland, Superintendent E. F. Moveton (1904–1905) states that "Of the eight teachers appointed to teach special classes, six had had large and successful experience in the State Institution [p. 104]."

The profession of music education was well established by 1900 and music had taken its place in the public schools as part of the common core of learnings. The programs, mostly vocal, were graded in difficulty from first grade through secondary school. The two basic goals of music educators during the first decade of the twentieth century were (1) to teach as many songs as possible in a given school year, and (2) to teach music reading where this was possible. Music education in the special classes concentrated upon the former, with students learning a great many songs by rote. The makeup of the classes was almost totally male, and military-like marching and singing techniques, passed down from the singing schools through the institutions, were the accepted practice. Toward the end of the first decade of the twentieth century the marching-and-singing practice began to give way to the rise of male glee clubs. The special-class glee clubs became the primary indicator of success of some special classes and they were often called upon with pride to perform in the community. The membership in special-class glee clubs increased significantly around the country as the compulsory education laws of the various states came into effect.

By the middle 1920s teacher-training textbooks and treatises on the feebleminded and other handicapped children almost universally recommended music as an essential part of special class curricula. The arguments for music experiences were almost always based upon practical educational values rather than esthetic needs. The writing of the Englishman Tredgold (1922), who had a good deal of influence upon American special educators, reflects this sentiment in his statement regarding the value of music for improving hearing of the feebleminded:

> Probably the best means of developing this faculty is by music. Singing, musical drill, and the concerts of the entertainment hall . . . not only develop the child's power of attention and the range and accuracy of his hearing, but are a source of greatest happiness [p. 479].

Tredgold also believed that musical experiences would be beneficial in speech training:

> In many cases where the faculty of speech lingers, music is a great help. As Dr. Shuttleworth says, "Such children will frequently hum tunes that take their fancy before they are able to articulate words; but if attractive tunes set to words containing repetitions of simple sounds (such as Baba Black Sheep of our old nursery rhymes) are constantly repeated to them, the probability is that, after a time, first one word and then another will be taken up by the pupil, til the rhyme as well as the tune is known. . . . Where muscular action is defective . . . it may be cultivated by encouraging the child to make use of his lips and tongue in blowing a toy trumpet or whistle [p. 484].

The deemphasis of enjoyment or esthetic pleasure in favor of learning through music is stressed by Spilman (1925) for training the feebleminded in religion:

> Music holds an important place in religious training. The feebleminded enjoy singing. Those who can, do it well. The message of the song, when lodged in the mind may be doing silent work in the still hours of the night. Snatches of the song sung by the pupils at their play may make of them teachers of their followers. Music through the ages had had an important place in the training of multitudes of people. Select songs with sound religious truths in them and drill and drill some more until many songs find a permanent lodgement. They will abide when oral instruction has gone [p. 251].

Emphasis on drill and the good results which might in some way help to alleviate difficulties associated with the child's handicapping condition continued to be the basis for music in the special classroom. This argument was voiced even more strongly by the proponents of music in the special class during the Great Depression of the thirties. During this period of great difficulty in financing any of the nation's schools, there was much talk about doing away with the "frills." The spirit of the times would not have permitted music to be retained as a special class offering if many had not been convinced of its unique value as an aid to learning by handicapped children.

There were reports of various kinds of learnings and social adaptations of handicapped children through music experiences in special education literature as well as that of music education. Some of the claims were clearly exaggerated and without benefit of being based upon controlled research. In their enthusiasm to justify the expense of music teachers for the handicapped, classroom teachers, music educators, and special educators at one time or another used music of some form in every part of the special education course and subject offerings. One could find music to teach counting, speaking, drawing, writing, and so forth. Walsh (1947) seems to put the entire movement into better perspective in the following statement:

> For, as big a contribution as it makes, it is not music alone, nor any other tool alone working with a magic phenomenon, but rather the predetermined goals set with it; the carefully planned and executed use of it by qualified persons, and the follow-up and support of its effect on the total child [p. 30].

Walsh's statement represents the view of many in the 1950s who wanted and worked for better planning and teaching in the special education programs of the nation. There was support for better programming for the handicapped by such groups as the newly formed National Association for Retarded Citizens. Over thirty states enacted laws that would provide direct subsidies for special education programs for exceptional children.

In 1958 Carey (1958) made a survey of music education programs in special education classes in cities with populations over 25,000. The purpose of the study was to determine the most effective and profitable types of music education for the mentally retarded. Carey also established nine field studies in northern Illinois in grades ranging from primary through junior high school. The field studies lasted four months under the direction of the investigator with the assistance of the classroom teachers involved.

Carey reported the following findings:

1. Music was included in the curricula for the mentally retarded in 458 of the 465 cities surveyed.
2. The mentally retarded children were taught with the same methodology as normal children but at a slower pace with more repetition.
3. Music education methods included singing by rote, listening activities, rhythms, eurhythmics, and rhythm band activities.
4. It appeared that mentally retarded children progressed in music at about the same rate as they progressed in other school subjects.

In a statement summarizing the status of music education in special education programs for the mentally retarded, Kirk (1964) writes:

Some forms of art and music activities are usually standard practices in educational programs for the mentally retarded. Research and evaluation of the effects of such activities are meager [p. 90].

Almost as if in response to the statement by Kirk, the literature of several disciplines, including music education and special education, started in the mid-1950s to reflect research on the use of music and other arts in the education and training of the handicapped. Much of the research that pertains to music with the handicapped has been indexed in the *Music Therapy Index* (Eagle, 1976). The Congress of the United States indicated an awareness of the value of music as a means of teaching handicapped youngsters in the development of the concept of "Free Appropriate Public Education" from Public Law 94-142. Under Section 121 a.304 of the Final Regulations, entitled "Full Educational Opportunity Goal," is the following:

Comment: In meeting the full educational opportunity goal, the Congress also encouraged local educational agencies to include artistic and cultural activities in programs supported under this part, subject to the priority requirements under 121a.320–121a.324. This point is addressed in the following statements from the Senate Report on Public Law 94-142:

The use of the arts as a teaching tool for the handicapped has long been recognized as a viable effective way not only of teaching special skills, but also of reaching youngsters who had otherwise been unteachable. The Committee envisions that programs under this bill could well include an arts component and, indeed, urges that local educational agencies include the arts in programs for the handicapped funded under this Act. Such a program could cover both appreciation of the arts by the handicapped youngsters and the utilization of the arts as a teaching tool per se.

The statements from P.L. 94-142 reflect another in the several steps of the history of music education of the handicapped from the early days of the New England institutions in the first decades of the nineteenth century. Through use of techniques developed in the colonial singing schools to improve singing in worship services, music experiences for the handicapped developed through the nineteenth-century institutions and were taken in toto into the special-education classes of the first decade of the twentieth century. For the next seventy-eight years, the special resource room music program was to be the primary means of experiencing music for the vast majority of the nation's handicapped who received any form of education at all. It has already been suggested that some of the music education claims and practices in far too many of these special rooms became suspect after close scrutiny by concerned persons. These individuals questioned the entire special-room phenomenon and vigorously opposed the fundamental concept of segregated school experiences for the handicapped.

By the mid 1960s there was mounting evidence that the special classes had become "dumping grounds" for unruly nonhandicapped children or for racially and culturally different children. Documented evidence of such misuse of the special class in an unfortunate number of instances became available. Consequently citizens began to use the courts and other means of bringing about change in the way that handicapped children would be educated. One result of such intervention by groups and individuals has been the movement toward mainstreaming and away from the special class. For music educators and other professional educators, one obvious problem is how to deal with the changes brought about by this new orientation to education of the handicapped in the regular music education class.

MUSIC EDUCATION OF THE HANDICAPPED AT THE IMPLEMENTATION DATE OF P.L. 94-142

With a few notable exceptions, professional music educators tended to ignore the special classes until the late 1960s and early 1970s. It has already been indicated that music was taught in these special rooms but usually by the special-education teachers. In some instances these teachers did superior jobs of music education, but for the most part, handicapped children did not benefit from the attentions of the professional music educator. In the early 1970s more and more music educators were assigned to special rooms primarily as a result of the increased attention that handicapped children were getting nationwide and because of the growing influence of special educators whose demands for the assistance of music specialists began to be heard. Still the attention given to the special rooms by the professional music educator was minimal. Typically, a music educator visited such a class two or three times a month for twenty-minute sessions of limited singing, listening to recordings, and limited rhythms or movement experiences. This type of activity was virtually ineffective as music education because of the small amount of actual teaching. It might not have produced significantly better results than the typical music session in resource rooms. Typically these sessions offered limited music experiences based on commercial "special education" recordings that directed the children through certain movements to music, usually at a rate of speed to which few students, handicapped or not, could accurately respond. The major part of all music education for the handicapped was on the elementary level, whereas handicapped children in the secondary grades were universally neglected or consciously excluded from music education experiences.

Based upon informal surveys from eight city systems and four rural systems selected from representative regions of the United States, it can be estimated that approximately one-third of the handicapped children receiving special education and related services of any kind were receiving some form of music education at the close of the 1977–1978 school year. Approximately half of these children were being taught by certified music educators, usually on an informally scheduled basis, frequently during "compensatory time" for the classroom teacher. A fair estimate, then, of handicapped children who were receiving music education at the implementation date of P.L. 94-142 is approximately 1,250,000 of the 3.7 million receiving any kind of special education and related services. This number equals about 15 percent of the total number of 7,887,000 * handicapped children in the United States served and unserved by special education and related services. An informal survey of music educators and administrators in the United States suggests that the availability of music education to handicapped children tends to follow the pattern of the "Percentage of Total Served" in the following table of data from the Bureau of Education for the Handicapped of the U.S. Office of Education. Speech-impaired children receive the most music education offered in regular music settings, with the deaf (not the visually impaired) receiving the least amount of music education.

Number of Children Receiving Special Education and Related Services by Reporting Category and Handicapping Condition

Handicapping Condition	P.L. 89-313	P.L. 94-142	Total	Percentage of Total Served
Speech-impaired	0	1,309,020	1,309,020	35.2
Mentally retarded	131,487	840,257	971,744	26.1
Learning-disabled	0	799,593	799,593	21.5
Emotionally disturbed	30,378	254,007	284,385	7.6
Other health-impaired	16,107	125,449	141,556	3.8
Deaf and hard of hearing	27,522	62,222	89,744	2.4
Orthopedically impaired (crippled)	8,413	78,889	87,302	2.3
Visually handicapped	9,925	28,539	38,464	1.0
TOTAL	223,832	3,497,976	3,721,808	99.9 *

* Note: The percentages do not total 100 because of rounding.

* The figure 7,887,000 handicapped children in the U.S. is projected from data available from the U.S. Office of Education, Bureau of Education for the Handicapped.

As of September 1, 1978, music educators and all other educators became subject to the national policy put forth in Public Law 94-142. After that date it was no longer permissible for school administrators or others to exclude handicapped children on the grounds that they could not learn, their handicaps were too severe, or that there were no programs for the problems in question. Abeson and Zettel (1977) state the case very well:

> The right to education also means that children with handicaps are eligible for participation in all programs and activities provided or sponsored by the schools as all other children are eligible. The presence of a handicap no longer can mean automatic ineligibility for music, athletics, cheerleading, or other extracurricular activities [p. 122].

Music educators are now faced with the problem of teaching the handicapped child, an issue that has been long ignored by members of the profession. Until the mid to late 1970s there were virtually no music-education methods classes to prepare prospective music educators to teach children with handicaps. It was assumed by music-education teacher training programs that music educators would be concerned with only the talented and highly motivated. Now it is incumbent upon music educators to deal with children in music education classes whether they are motivated or not and regardless of handicap. This will undoubtedly mean changes in some of the traditional approaches to music education. These changes do not necessarily mean that music offerings need be less meaningful or less educative. On the contrary, mainstreaming may come as a blessing in disguise forcing music educators to think and plan innovatively to develop better and more effective means of musically educating all of the children assigned to him or her.

It can be seen that music education of the handicapped has a history as old as concern for the handicapped in the United States. The trends in teaching methodology have reflected the attitudes toward the handicapped and the settings in which they have been served. Whatever the means of teaching or training, music has been considered a good experience. As the country moved toward the passage of P.L. 94-142, more and more professionally prepared music educators began to teach music to the handicapped although less than a third of these students were being taught by music educators at the September 1, 1978 date of implementation of the Act. At this point the music educator, special educator, regular class teachers, parents, and others concerned with music education of the handicapped face problems similar to those of educators in other disciplines. There is concern now with how music education might best be offered to handicapped children who need special education and related services to learn music, particularly, in mainstreaming situations or in other environments deemed most conducive to learning. The following pages are concerned with development of objectives for the individualized educational program in music. A special effort has been made to provide guidelines for developing music programs that will assure that, to the maximum extent appropriate, handicapped children will experience music education in regular educational environments. Such an approach is consistent with the Act's concept of the least restrictive alternative.

2 Guidelines for Developing Individualized Educational Programs in Music

THE INDIVIDUALIZED EDUCATIONAL PROGRAM IN MUSIC

It should be made clear from the beginning of this discussion that the simple fact of physical or mental anomaly does not necessarily mean that a child will require the federally mandated individualized educational program (IEP) in music. When a physical or mental variance offers no hindrance to classroom study of music, a child with such a variance must be considered to be nonhandicapped, at least as far as his music education is concerned. Such a child, regardless of his physical appearance, should be taught music in the same way that any nonhandicapped child would be taught.

The individualized educational program in music will be developed for a child who requires special education or related services in order to study music in school or in whatever environment is determined "least restrictive" by the developers of that child's individualized educational program in music. When the IEP is to be developed by a music educator or when the music educator acts as a contributing consultant to the classroom teacher, there are certain procedures which should be followed. What follows is information to provide music educators, administrators, teachers, and parents with a set of procedures for planning individualized education programs in music which will meet the requirements of Public Law 94-142.

The Education for All Handicapped Children Act of 1975 (Public Law 94-142) specifies that all "handicapped" children who need to receive special education and related services will be provided with a written individualized program (IEP). According to this Act, the IEP should include the following:

> A written statement for each handicapped child developed in any meeting by a representative of the local educational agency or an intermediate educational unit who shall be qualified to provide, or supervise the provision of, specially designed instruction to meet the unique needs of handicapped children, the teacher, the parents or guardians of such child, and whenever appropriate, such child, which statement shall include (A) a statement of the present levels of educational performance of such child, (B) a statement of annual goals including short-term instructional objectives, (C) a statement of the specific educational services to be provided to such child, and the extent to which such child will be able to participate in regular educational programs, (D) the projected date for initiation and anticipated duration of such services and appropriate objective criteria and evaluation procedures and schedules for determining, on at least an annual basis, whether instructional objectives are being achieved.

It is important for the music educator to be aware of the fact that each local education agency is required to develop or revise an individualized education program for every handicapped child at the beginning of the school year. The music educator should make it a point to be on hand when the IEP is being developed. Federal policy requires that at least three persons be present, a representative of the local education agency, the child's teacher (or teachers), and at least one of the parents. When appropriate, the child should be present. The music educator should attend the development conference as one of the child's teachers. If the music educator is not present, it is probable that unrealistic music goals will be set for the child, if, indeed, any goals at all are set.

ASSESSMENT

The individuals who meet to develop the IEP are required to put in writing a statement of the child's present levels of educational performance and a statement describing the child's learning style.

Initially, the local education agency will be required to conduct assessment to certify that a particular child is eligible to receive special education or related services. During this period of assessment the music educator should prepare a statement describing the child's present levels of (general) performance in all areas of classroom music-education activities—that is, singing, playing instruments, moving rhythmically, listening (and describing what is heard), and reading and creating music.

It is the intent of Public Law 94-142 that assessment information should be collected on an individual-child basis, that "assessments should be individualized according to the child's presenting behavior." The music educator should begin with any information currently on file regarding the child's music behaviors. This information might have been collected previously by the music educator or might come from the records of a previous music educator. Such information not only is valuable in determining the present level of music performance, but it can also be useful for determining hearing and visual difficulties. All such information will contribute to the suggestion that "assessment information come from multiple sources."

The music education assessment should not be culturally or linguistically biased. A child can be evaluated for singing ability regardless of the language in which he or she sings or the style in which the singing is done. Nonbiased assessment of linguistically different children would be concerned solely with the act of singing—that is, the ability to sustain a singing tone, intonation (taking style into account), phrasing, and so forth.

The music-education assessment should be sensitive to the child's handicapping condition. The music educator should make a conscious effort to evaluate the strengths, at least the normal aspects, of the handicapped child's music behavior. For example, if the child has poor hearing, the pitch-matching parts of some of the standardized music tests should be abandoned in favor of tests evaluating the child's movement and rhythmic abilities. With mainstreaming in mind, the music educator will assess the handicapped child in terms of that child's performance in a music class of relatively nonhandicapped children. Although each child must be assessed in an individualized manner and a program developed in terms of that child's particular music-education needs, there should be some point of reference to facilitate planning and teaching. The *Music Education Assessment Sheet* shown on page 20 and the *Developmental Schedule for Music Behaviors* on pages 28–32 are two instruments that can be used in assessing music behaviors of handicapped children and planning annual goals. The *Music Education Assessment Sheet* was developed by the authors and music educators from the state of North Carolina. It affords the music educator the means of assessing music behaviors as they might be developed in mainstreaming conditions or in a resource room setting (whichever is determined as "least restrictive").

Music Education Assessment Sheet

2 = regular music class placement
1 = would progress best in resource or special room setting
0 = cannot perform the task at present

		ALONE	WITH OTHERS	WITH MUSICAL ACCOMPANIMENT	Scores
Singing	Familiar Song				
	Harmony Part				
	Sight-reads				
Playing Instruments	Rhythm Instr.				
	Chordal-fretted				
	Melodic-percussive				
Rhythmic Response	To Words				
	To Beat in Music				
	To Subdivision of Beat				
Describing Music	Same vs. Different				
	Loud vs. Quiet				
	Fast vs. Slow by Bodily Movement				
Creative Response/ Expression	Bodily				
	Vocal				
	Instrumental				
	Graphic				

TOTAL _____

Related Services:
1. Adapted Musical Instruments _____
2. Transportation _____
3. Hearing or Visual Aids _____
4. Other _____

Statement of Present Level of Performance in Music: _____
_____
_____
_____

20

LONG-TERM (ANNUAL) GOALS

In order to write appropriate goals in music education, the planners must begin with where the child is musically at the time of planning. Although the music educator should take the lead in determining these goals, everyone involved in the development of the IEP must agree to the final written statement. This means that the parents, teachers, administrators, music educator, and, when appropriate, the child must decide on a "best estimate" of what the child will be able to do in music at the end of the academic year.

The following two examples of annual goals for the music education of handicapped children derive from "present level of performance statements" and represent fairly low music functioning skills.

> *Present Level of Performance:* Attempts to use singing voice but with little pitch or rhythmic accuracy.
>
> *Annual Goals:* (a) Will sing a short song evidencing pitch and rhythmic approximations; (b) Will sing with one or more other children maintaining the proper beat and following melodic contours.
>
> *Present Level of Performance:* Attempts to clap in accompaniment to music but shows little, if any, response to major pulse patterns.
>
> *Annual Goals:* (a) Will clap the major beat in each measure to rhythmically simple duple music; (b) Will step to simple martial music played on the piano.

AFFECTIVE ESTHETIC GOALS IN THE IEP

An obvious shortcoming in the Education for All Handicapped Children Act of 1975 is the failure to emphasize the importance of effective esthetic education for the handicapped. The music educator might often be the only member of the IEP development team who can offer definite suggestions for the esthetic education of the handicapped child.

One problem is the requirement to develop goals from assessment of the child's presenting behaviors. The question for the planners of the IEP in music is, What are esthetic behaviors, and how can they be assessed? Perhaps even more difficult is stating how the child should behave esthetically at the end of a school year.

Esthetic behaviors should be assessed in the five areas already mentioned: singing, playing instruments, listening, moving to music, and creating music. Some examples of annual goals derived from present-level statements represent emerging to low esthetic performance levels:

> *Present Level of Performance:* The child sings more loudly than anyone else in the class, with very little responsiveness to cues for changes in dynamics.

Annual Goals: (a) Will sing in a manner that will permit her voice to blend with those of the remainder of the class. (b) Will respond to conductor's cues and dynamic markings on printed page of music.

Present Level of Performance: Will listen to music only when permitted to moan, groan, and make other utterances.

Annual Goal: Will listen to music in relative silence, making no more extraneous noise than other members of the class.

SPECIAL EDUCATIONAL SERVICES TO FACILITATE MUSIC EDUCATION OF THE HANDICAPPED

The language of P.L. 94-142 requires that each individualized educational program contain a statement of educational services needed by the child (determined without regard to the availability of those services), including a description of

1. All special education and related services needed to meet the unique needs of the child, including the type of physical education program in which the child will participate.
2. Any special instructional media and materials that are needed (121a225)

It should be made clear that with regard to music education of handicapped children one would be required to list *only* highly specialized material or media that related directly to the child's own need in music.

Examples of such material might be especially large note heads on sheet music for visually impaired children, specially adapted musical instruments, hearing aids adapted for music listening and movement activities, and the like. The individual or individuals responsible for achieving the annual goals should be listed also. In the case of mildly handicapped children, this is likely to be the music educator or the regular classroom teacher with support from an itinerant music educator.

SHORT-TERM INSTRUCTIONAL OBJECTIVES

Several short-term instructional objectives must be written into the IEP for each annual goal in music education. The short-term objectives are increments in progress of music learning from the child's present level to his or her annual goals. The number of short-term objectives will be determined by the music educator and the remainder of the IEP development committee as a part of the examination of the goals. It would appear that in most instances three or four short-term objectives for each annual goal would be sufficient.

Take, for example, an annual goal presented earlier:

The child will sing a short song evidencing pitch and rhythmic approximations.

Short-term instructional objectives might be

1. To match a pitch sung by the teacher or music educator
2. To repeat a phrase sung by the teacher
3. To sing an eight-measure song with classmates
4. To sing an eight-measure song alone

In writing the short-term objectives it is not necessary to list each aspect of every step between initial assessment and the annual goal. Short-term instructional objectives are not intended to be lesson plans. During the course of the academic year the music educator may break the sequence of increments into smaller steps, which may be done without reconvening the development committee or rewriting the IEP.

Music educators and others should keep the following two points in mind when writing annual music education goals and objectives for handicapped children:

1. Anticipations for growth in musical skill and knowledge should neither be so easy as to become boring nor so difficult that they lead to frustration.
2. Anticipations for growth should be broad enough in scope to permit unexpected gains in any one or all five of the areas of music learning (i.e., singing, playing, listening, moving, creating).

PARENTAL INVOLVEMENT

When assessment has indicated that the student requires special education to benefit from the music curriculum of his school, the parents become obligated to participate in planning music-education goals of the IEP. When the student has been assessed, the parents should meet with the professionals who conducted the assessment to discuss the outcomes. If the parents are not pleased, a reassessment can be requested. Parents may request to be present at any assessment of their child.

If the results of the assessment are acceptable, one or both parents are expected to meet with the classroom teacher, authorized school administrator, and music educator to prepare long-term goals and short-term instructional objectives for the student. At this meeting the parent should be prepared to describe the child's music behavior at home and to indicate something of the child's main interests and talents, particularly if this information is not reflected in the assessment outcomes.

It is important for parents to remember that music (and other arts) education has been recognized by the framers of P.L. 94-142 as being required to meet the "full educational opportunity goal" of each handicapped child (121a. 304). Furthermore, parents should be aware of the fact that practically every child is capable of benefiting from music education regardless of the severity of any handicapping condition. As an active member of the IEP development committee, parents can see to it that their children will receive any special methodology or needed educational services to ensure the musical growth and development of their child.

MUSIC EDUCATION IN THE LEAST RESTRICTIVE ENVIRONMENT

The needed educational services serve one basic concept as set forth in P.L. 94-142, that of the "least restrictive environment." Ideally, the needed related educational services will facilitate learning in the regular music class by the handicapped child. When such mainstreaming is deemed inappropriate, and the child's individual needs require removal from the regular music program for "special music education" or for the provision of related services, that removal must be documented. As indicated in the law, documentation of educational services must include

1. A description of the extent to which the child will participate in regular (music) education programs
2. A justification for the type of (music) educational placement the child will have

EVALUATION

Public Law 94-142 sets forth requirements for evaluation data under two separate sections of the Act. With specific reference to individualized education programs, the law calls for

appropriate objective criteria and evaluation procedures and schedules for determining, at least on an annual basis, whether instructional objectives are being achieved [121a 47].

Individualized education programs in music for handicapped children must be evaluated to meet the general evaluation requirements of P.L. 94-142. Observable, *objective criteria* are necessary to determine whether the child has accomplished the short-term instructional objectives in music. Criteria for demonstrating accomplishment of music tasks are integral parts of the statements of objectives found later in this book.

Appropriate objective criteria for evaluating music education objectives should be agreed upon during the planning of the program or shortly thereafter. Perhaps the most efficient means of accomplishing this aspect of the evaluation requirements is collecting progress data of the handicapped children for whom the program has been planned.

DATA-KEEPING PROCEDURES
IN THE MUSIC CLASS

The very idea of keeping data on the progress of handicapped children might at first appear to many music educators to be a burdensome bit of additional busywork. Upon further consideration, however, most would agree that periodic charting of student progress is likely to be the best means of accomplishing the task. Evaluation of handicapped children is made relatively uncomplicated by a process consisting of the following steps in gathering data:

1. The short-term instructional objectives should be written in behavioral terms and should include a criterion statement whenever feasible. For example: "The student will clap two beats to the measure of a thirty-two-measure instrumental selection with no less than 80 percent accuracy."

2. Base-line data, a pre-music-education picture of the child's music behavior, should be charted as a basis for comparison of behaviors after music education experiences. Generally, there should be at least three observations of the behavior in question. For the clapping example above, the teacher might observe the student attempting to clap to the specified musical selection on three different classroom occasions.

3. The music-education program is then started. The clapping example would reflect progress of the child over some specified period; he would be evaluated as to his ability to clap to thirty-two measures. The evaluation should be done on some sort of consistent periodical basis.

4. During the course of the music-education experiences, the music educator should constantly evaluate the effectiveness of the program, subjectively as well as objectively. If progress is sufficient to justify continuation of the student in the program this is done; if progress is insufficient, an immediate reevaluation of the program is mandatory.

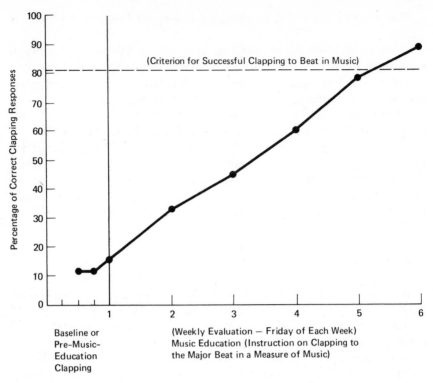

Figure 2-1 *Short-term Instructional Objective:* John will clap two beats to the measure of a thirty-two-measure instrumental selection with no less than 80 percent accuracy.

The progress data for the example cited above could be charted in the manner shown in Figure 2–1.

DESIRABILITY OF CRITERION-REFERENCED MEASUREMENT

Many traditional music education programs in the country are test-oriented and involve comparisons with other class members. Examples are the "music aptitude" tests to qualify aspiring band members. The results of such tests are recorded as percentiles, standard scores as percentages with no interpretation for diagnostic purposes. The atmosphere of the "challenge" system for chair ranks in bands, for example, stresses competition over individual growth. Arguments could be made that such an evaluation procedure is inherently discriminatory (designed to select the "highest music aptitude") and is used with no intention of program adjustment. Such a procedure is test-oriented and norm-referenced and frequently unrelated to child needs in music education.

What is required is that music educators become much more concerned with objectives of instruction in music and develop evaluation procedures that are clearly related to the areas of music instruction (i.e., singing, playing, moving, creating, listening).

As the music educator becomes more aware of the five areas of music instruction and becomes more capable of appropriately representing these areas in teacher-made test items, norm-referenced procedures become less essential to the music education process.

This is not to suggest that there is no place for some of the currently popular commercial music tests. On the other hand, the music educator is encouraged to include informal observations. When norm-referenced testing is employed, let the students take part in any comparison of their efforts with the "so-called" national norms. Finally, the music educator needs always to remember that the primary purposes of assessment and evaluation are to provide a basis for program planning and that assessment and evaluation must always be related directly to the child and to his individual music education program.

DEVELOPMENTAL SCHEDULES
FOR GUIDEPOSTS

Criterion-referenced testing suggests a test–music education–retest paradigm which permits the teacher and often the handicapped child to focus more sharply on weak areas that need strengthening. Knowledge of the pattern of development of music behaviors will assist the music educator in selecting areas which may be weak or strong as a basis for planning the music-education program. The developmental schedule on pages 28–32 is an approximation of the developmental pattern of music behaviors from ages one through eleven. The schedules are not presented as rigid matrices or unwavering paths but as a general sequence of the appearance of singing and manipulative skills and, subsequently, of music-making abilities. These schedules should be helpful in developing annual goals for handicapped and nonhandicapped children alike in mainstreaming situations for music educators.

SAMPLE INDIVIDUAL EDUCATION PROGRAM

On pages 33–40 are four examples of individualized educational programs. The first two show music as a component in the classroom IEP and consequently include several areas of growth. The third and fourth examples are designed for music instruction and therefore emphasize one subject area: music.

Development Schedule for Music Behaviors

Developmental Characteristics Of Music Behaviors	Music Age (in Years)	Suggested Activities for Music Education
1. Follows simple instructions—gurgles, coos to music and songs of adults. Walks with two-hand support. Claps hands in glee (not on the beat) when music is heard.	1:00	Adult sings short phrases requiring physical response by the child. Uses melodies of two or three pitches that give instructions: "Stand up" (e¹g); "sit up" (e¹g); "sit down" (g e); "turn around" (e e g); and so forth.
2. Recognizes and points to body parts when parts are sung about in a song. Expressive vocabulary of 10 or more words. Spontaneous humming or singing from loud to soft over span of an octave. Total bodily response to music stimuli (vocal or instrumental). Where is your hair? Where is your nose? Where is your mouth? Where are your eyes? Etc.	1:50	Adult sings longer phrases about familiar body parts, to which the child points. There it is! There they are! (Take child's hand and point)
3. Talks and sings in short phrases, generally not on pitch. Can relate songs to a few common pictures. Enjoys rocking, swinging, bending, swaying, and tapping feet to music. Enjoys walking (not on beat) to music. Fascinated by various sound sources.	2:00	Individual and group music activities using large colored pictures to stimulate singing. Short phrases related to pictures. Parent or teacher should sing nursery rhymes with and without musical accompaniment (piano, guitar, ukulele).

2:50 Encourage singing. Let child feel face and jaws of adult singers. Let them experiment with the piano. Encourage movement to a variety of rhythmic patterns. Play call-and-response games using child's fifty-word vocabulary. Use common pronouns.

3:00 No concentrated music activity should exceed eight minutes. When listening to music, visual guides to melody and rhythm should be provided. The musical concepts of loud-soft, fast-slow; same-different can be introduced through physical movement. Much singing and movement to music.

3:50 Sing songs using newly mastered m, p, b, h, and w sounds. Encourage the child to sing stories relating personal experiences. Use many finger plays and musical games which employ musical cues for movement change of direction, stopping, etc.

4:00 Model and encourage good singing habits. Permit and encourage small group and solo singing. Have child imitate "body sounds" and make up sounds with his body. Experiment with environmental sounds. Introduce Orff xylophones on pentatonic scale, drums, and other percussion instruments.

5:00 Introduce new songs to increase song repertory. Song dramatizations should be encouraged. Circle singing games should be taught. Opportunities should be made available for creative use of singing voice, body movements, and musical instruments.

4. May have learned parts of several songs from parents, TV, radio, recordings. Singing not on pitch or beat. Spontaneous singing, frequent use of smaller intervals (including the minor third). Enjoys running, galloping, swinging, swaying to music (not yet on the beat). Enjoys simple circle games such as Ring-around-the-Rosy, London Bridge.

5. Can reproduce entire short songs, not yet on pitch. Can match pitches sung by an adult. Will sing "Happy Birthday," Christmas carols, Sunday school hymns in a group. Can walk, run, jump and gallop in character with music, not always on the beat.

6. Sings a few nursery rhymes alone with most of the essential details of pitch rhythm, although not necessarily the "given" pitch, or tempo. Can execute finger plays. Tendency to maintain tonal center if not good intonation.

7. Singing voice rapidly developing. Some entire songs sung on pitch and with correct rhythm. Can sing in groups but enjoys solo singing. Loves to experiment with musical sounds. Recognizes many tunes by name. Enjoys Orff and rhythm instruments.

8. Singing voice small but shows characteristic ("fluty" or "reedy") quality. Can sing several short songs on pitch with good rhythm and pulse. High interest in dramatizing songs. Increased spontaneity in rhythms; can move many ways in character of music heard.

Development Schedule for Music Behaviors—Continued

Developmental Characteristics Of Music Behaviors	Music Age (in Years)	Suggested Activities for Music Education
9. Singing voice still small but clearly developing. With the proper early childhood experiences behind him, he may sing frequently alone, with others, to recordings, television, or radio, and with parents. He can learn to play a few familiar songs on the piano. Enjoys dancing to music but cannot always step to the beat, particularly to slower pulses.	5:50	Use rote teaching-learning method to introduce children to singing games, chants, and nursery rhymes not already learned. Instruct children on how to listen and what to listen for in short recorded and live musical presentations. Permit the child to experiment with the piano. Introduce xylophone and drums for experimentation.
10. Those with kindergarten and nursery school singing experience have good singing voices. Children entering school for the first time may evidence uncertainty as singers. Children show evidence of being able to step to quick time marches or to a quick drumbeat.	6:00	Expand song repertory. Work individually with uncertain singers. Use solfeggio and hand signals with familiar songs to establish association with symbols and scale concepts. Introduce step or "ladder" bells. Encourage individual musical performance. Encourage repetition of rhythmic patterns on drums and through bodily movement.
11. The child is able to match pitches well and sing back simple songs after a few hearings. Still plays piano, xylophone with favored hand; has difficulty with two-hand coordination of mallets, drums, triangles, maracas, etc. Can run to a major pulse if the tempo is adapted to the child's running pace.	6:50	Encourage rote singing of longer songs; large notation on lined chalkboard or paper used alone and later in combination with hand signals to develop pitch-symbol concepts. Opportunities to use movement repertory to live and recorded music: swing, sway, bend to music followed by stepping and running to a clear, even pulse.
12. Good singing voices: well placed except in problem cases. Shows skill in imitating singing of teacher and other adults (TV, radio, recording personalities). Group singing takes on more importance. Can march steadily to pulses at various speeds. Runs, jumps, hops in character of the music. Shows good two-hand/eye coordination in playing rhythm instruments, Autoharp.	7:00	Sing chants and simple rounds. Other group singing in unison and simple harmony (descants, combination songs, canons). Circle games and folk dances using live and recorded "callers." Teach basics of music form: like and unlike patterns, phrases, "musical sentences," and so forth. Additional experience with pre-music-reading concepts such as high and low, fast and slow, and major and minor.

13. Children can hold one voice part while others sing in rounds, canons, and descants and can switch to harmony parts with assistance from the teacher. Child can execute all of movement repertory including skipping to $\frac{6}{8}$ time. Can perform in Orff Schulwerk ensembles.

7:50 Sing combination songs, canons, two- and three-part rounds. Add descants and chants to familiar tunes. Incorporate hand signals and written symbols with singing of familiar tunes. Sing from songbooks. Introduce more advanced folk dances including some non-Western ones. Provide ample opportunity to play Orff instruments.

14. Children can sing longer, more complex songs from songbooks. Ready use of hand signals and solfeggio possible at this age. Children can conduct any of the common meters. Increasing proficiency on percussion instruments. Autoharp can be played as accompaniment for self and class.

8:00 Teacher leads children through singing experiences directly related to notation and music reading. Conducting experiences should be provided. Advanced Orff Schulwerk and Dalcroze Eurhythmics. More complex folk dances and dramatic musical experiences should be taught. Accompaniment of singing from chord symbol or by ear on the Autoharp.

15. Strong singing voice reflects continuing development of vocal chords and lungs. Develops style of singing and personal preference for certain songs. Capable of fairly intricate dance steps and complex hand-eye tasks with instruments. Shows interests in orchestral and recreational musical instruments.

8:50 Provide many experiences with new and traditional songs over range of an octave. Rounds, canons, combination songs, descants, chants of medium complexity. Marching and playing experiences using rhythm instruments. Accompaniment experiences on Autoharp, ukulele, banjo, dulcimer. Song flutes, ocarinas, and slide whistles should be introduced.

16. Interest in singing "pop" tunes of the day. Is capable of singing almost anything the average adult can sing (boys an octave higher than men). Definite preferences for certain kinds of music. Understands meter differences, mode, modulation, dynamic changes. Ready to begin orchestral and band instruments, also guitar.

9:00 Provide individual and group singing experiences. Teach the use of fretted instruments as accompaniment. Many music reading experiences. Analysis of music heard and of music scores. Experiences with several meters, mixed meters, polytonality, etc. Introduce orchestral band and fretted instruments for individual study.

Development Schedule for Music Behaviors—Continued

Developmental Characteristics Of Music Behaviors	Music Age (in Years)	Suggested Activities for Music Education
17. Some students will have developed considerable interest in singing in youth choirs. Other children continue to sing what pop heroes sing. Various levels of skill are shown on musical instruments. Capable of intricate dance steps and eurhythmics of extended duration.	10:00	Expose children to a variety of singing styles by having them sing different kinds of music solos, and in small and larger ensembles. Need to build basic skills on instruments. Can use several chords on the Autoharp. Make use of movement/dance experiences to back form expression and rhythmic groupings in music.
18. Boys' voices beginning to drop an octave. Girls' voices become "fuller" in quality. Capable of singing two- and three-part music. Developing technique on musical instruments with some soloists very good at accompanying themselves on piano and guitar.	11:00	Introduce choral singing. Careful treatment of boys' "cambiata" voices. Extensive music-reading experiences. Private instruction on instruments if possible. Baton twirling; marching and playing experiences. Formal instruction in music on a "pre-music theory" basis. Many opportunities to hear different kinds of live and recorded music.

Individualized Education Program (Example 1)

STUDENT'S NAME (FIRST, LAST)			DATE OF BIRTH	PUPIL ID	
Johnny Smith			September 24, 1972	8-11-01	
SCHOOL		DISTRICT	IEP REVIEW DATE	TODAY'S DATE	
George Washington Elem. School		IV	Sept. 2, 1979	Sept. 2, 1978	
TEACHER(S)				GRADE/PROGRAM	
Ms. R. Jones; Ms. E. Kimbrough (Music)					

PRIMARY ASSIGNMENT(S)	STARTING DATE	EXPECTED DURATION OF SERVICE
Regular Class, First Grade		
Special Education, (Reading, Arithmetic)		
Music (Special Education)		
SERVICES		
Wheelchair, Transportation		

REASON FOR ASSIGNMENT(S):
Assessment revealed poor reading and inability to handle basic number

concepts. Music assessment shows minimal ability to sustain a singing

voice and very poor rhythmic abilities.

ADMINISTRATOR/SUPERVISOR RESPONSIBLE FOR PROGRAM (NAME AND TITLE)
Mr. V. Smith, Principal

ADDRESS	PHONE
George Washington Elementary School. 2nd and Cherry	765-4321

THE FOLLOWING PERSONS HAVE PARTICIPATED IN THE EDUCATIONAL PROGRAM PLANNING CONFERENCE:

SCHOOL DISTRICT REPRESENTATIVE (NAME AND TITLE)
Mr. V. Smith, Principal

TEACHER(S)
Mrs. R. Jones, 1st grade; Ms. E. Kimbrough, Music Consultant.

OTHERS
Mr. A. Wright, Educational Psychometrist

STUDENT	PARENT
Johnny Smith	Ms. Elizabeth Smith

PARENT RESPONSE: I ☒ DO ☐ DO NOT APPROVE OF THE INDIVIDUALIZED EDUCATION PROGRAM WHICH IS RECOMMENDED.

_____   _____
Signature of Parent   Date

Once you indicate approval, the program will be implemented.

If you disapprove of the educational placement or program recommended for the student, you may request a hearing to resolve any differences by checking the space provided for disapproval and signing your name. To request a hearing, you must send your request within 20 days of the date of the program planning conference. You must send in your request within 10 days if you received it by mail.

If you indicate disapproval, the program will not be implemented. No change in assignment will occur until the decision of the hearing officer is received. Please review the notice which was previously sent to you. It contains an outline of hearing procedures.

If you do not respond within 20 days of the program planning conference, it will indicate that you approve of the educational placement and program that was discussed at the conference and any revisions which are attached. No response also indicates that you waive the right to a hearing at this time.

S953 9/77 THE SCHOOL DISTRICT OF PHILADELPHIA

EDUCATIONAL LEVELS & OBJECTIVES

SCHOOL: George Washington Elem
STUDENT'S NAME: Johnny Smith

ASSESSMENT PROCEDURES	CURRICULAR AREA	DESCRIPTION OF PRESENT EDUCATIONAL LEVELS	DATE	PROGRAM PLANNER
Music assessment instrument	Music	Strength: Imitates short vocal sounds, shows an interest in music. Needs: To develop better rhythmic response: unable to tap feet to music. To sing phrases.	9/10	Ms. E. Kimbrough
Reading: Peabody Individual Assessment Test	Reading	Strengths: Recognizes letters, has good visual memory Needs: To work on letter sounds, blending		Ms. R. Jones
PT/OT/functional evaluation and Denver PT test	Gross Motor Skills	Leg turns inward, awkward ambulation, poor balance, arm strength is weak		Mr. T. Walls

ANNUAL GOALS

INSTRUCTIONAL AREA				PROGRAM PLANNER
Music	Will respond to music by tapping the feet/ and imitate short phrases			Ms. E. Kimbrough
Reading	Will improve letter sounds and blending to a criterion of at least 55%			Ms. R. Jones
Physical Education	Will show substantial growth in arm strength			Mr. T. Walls

SHORT TERM OBJECTIVES

SHORT TERM OBJECTIVES	ASSESSMENT PROCEDURES	PRE - TEST		POST - TEST	
		DATE	SCORE	DATE	SCORE
Will tap feet at the sound of a drum.	Will tap feet with the drum beat as teacher plays 16 measures of four four meter with 80% accuracy.				
Will imitate short vocal sounds in a song.	Will imitate short vocal sounds in two of three consecutive sessions.				
Will sound 5 letters correctly.					
Will increase strength in arms.					

Individualized Education Program (Example 2)

Present Level	Annual Goals	Specific Instructional Objectives	Evaluation Criteria	Materials–Strategies
Social–Emotional Development: No leadership skills displayed. Does not initiate activities; speaks very softly.	To develop leadership skills (especially speaking more loudly and developing ability to choose activities).	Orally presented with three different rhythm instrument activities, Jane will choose one activity and lead the class in that activity, giving directions in a loud and clear voice.	Teacher observation	Rhythm instrument activity requiring verbal directions of stop and start, fast and slow.
Academic: Does not demonstrate knowledge of the following spatial relationships: up and down and left and right.	To participate in music activities requiring understanding of the concepts left and right and up and down.	Given appropriate, simple folk dances, Harry will indicate understanding of the concepts left and right and up and down by performing the required actions with 100 percent accuracy.	Teacher observation	Simple folk dances chosen from the book *Music Activities for Retarded Children.*
Behavior: Unable to follow a short series of directions.	Sally will participate in a class music activity which	Sally will stamp her feet, clap her hands, turn	Teacher observation	Series of folk dances requiring an increasing

35

requires following a series of directions.	around, and walk with the group in a circle (holding hands) in response to the directions in the folk dance, "Chimes of Dunkirk" (in book *Music Activities for Retarded Children*).		number of directions starting with one direction and gradually progressing to five directions.
Visual–Motor: Unable to perform most tasks requiring high degree of eye–hand coordination.	Sam will accompany a short song played on the piano by using a mallet instrument appropriately. Sam will play a rhythmic accompaniment on the snare drum for the duration of the song, "When the Saints Go Marching In," using drumsticks appropriately.	Teacher observation	Start with heavy drumsticks and tympani beaters and gradually progress to sticks of regular size. Move from a drum with a large surface (Ex. kettledrum) to a snare drum.
Language: Speaks very softly with poor enunciation. Does not initiate verbalizations.	Gary will sing the words of a simple tune with improved enunciation. Gary will sing the words for the "Hello" song in response to a piano accompaniment.	Teacher observation	"Hello" song from Nordoff-Robbins first book of *Children's Play Songs*.
Motor: Moves very awkwardly when walking.	Steve will respond to a drumbeat by walking in the same rhythm as the drumbeats. Steve will walk across the room in response to a slow, steady beat played on the bass drum.	Teacher observation	Bass drum and beater, plus selections of recorded songs with slow, steady beat.

These IEP's were prepared by Joanne R. Warres, Registered Music Therapist, Baltimore (MD.) City Public Schools.

Individualized Education Program (Example 3)

1. Student	James King	2. Committee	Position	Initial Date
		Ms. J. Strong	Music Teacher	

School Paxton Elementary

Grade III

Ms. J. Strong — Music Teacher

Dr. T. Forman — Asst. Prin.

Current Placement Resource Room

Ms. J. Kane — Resource Teacher

Date of birth 8/7/69 **Age** 9

3. Present Level of Functioning

Strengths: Plays rhythm instruments quite well, maintains rhythm most of the time. Can imitate simple sounds.

Needs: To improve use of his singing voice. To improve his ability to respond to music rhythmically in a less inhibited manner.

4. Annual Goal

Will imitate short phrases in songs.

Will respond by running, synchronizing his steps to the drumbeat.

5. Instructional Objective

Will imitate a short random phrase.

Will respond to a fast drumbeat by running, though not necessarily synchronizing steps with beat.

6. Assessment Procedure

Will imitate the phrase accurately in pitch and rhythm in two of three consecutive sessions.

Will run to the drumbeat (sixteen measures of $\frac{4}{4}$) with 80 percent accuracy.

7. Educational Services to be Provided

a. Services required

A full-frequency-range hearing aid. Music in a regular classroom having a hard surface floor.

Sixteen twenty-minute sessions with the music therapists to develop the singing voice and synchronize running movement with the drumbeat.

b. Date initiated

10/1/78

c. Duration

8 weeks

d. Individual response

Joan Reed

e. Extent of time in regular educational program.

Placed in the regular third-grade music class one thirty-minute period per week.

f. Justification for placement

Placement based on music-assessment instrument.

8. I have had the opportunity to participate in the development of this individualized education program.

Parent's signature _____

37

Individualized Education Program (Example 4)

Name _____   Teacher _____   Date _____

EACH AREA OF THE MULTIPLE CRITERIA LISTED MUST BE ADDRESSED: GENERAL HEALTH; MOTOR; LANGUAGE; VISUAL MOTOR; BEHAVIOR; SOCIAL/EMOTIONAL DEVELOPMENT; ACADEMIC ACHIEVEMENT.

Present Level of Performance	Annual Goals	Specific Instructional Objectives	Evaluation Criteria	Projected Date of Mastery	Materials/Strategy and/or Techniques
AT PRESENT THE STUDENT IS PERFORMING AT LEVEL ____ IN MUSIC SKILLS.	TO INCREASE THE STUDENT'S PERFORMANCE IN MUSIC SKILLS TO A LEVEL OF ____ .	THE STUDENT WILL DEMONSTRATE HIS/HER ABILITY TO INTERPRET MUSIC NOTATION PERFORMING AT A LEVEL OF ____, TWO VOCAL OR INSTRUMENTAL COMPOSITIONS OF CONTRASTING STYLE.			Modality Strengths _____ _____ Modality Weaknesses _____ _____
LEVEL 1 0-20% accuracy					MUSIC ELEMENTS PROVIDED IN THE COMPOSITION'S NOTATION (THOSE CIRCLED)
LEVEL 2 20-40% accuracy					RHYTHM
LEVEL 3 40-60% accuracy					MELODY
LEVEL 4 60-80% accuracy					TONE COLOR
LEVEL 5 80-100% accuracy					HARMONY
					TEXTURE
					FORM AND STYLE

EACH AREA OF THE MULTIPLE CRITERIA LISTED MUST BE ADDRESSED: GENERAL HEALTH; MOTOR; LANGUAGE; VISUAL MOTOR; BEHAVIOR; SOCIAL/EMOTIONAL DEVELOPMENT; ACADEMIC ACHIEVEMENT.

Present Level of Performance	Annual Goals	Specific Instructional Objectives	Evaluation Criteria	Projected Date of Mastery	Materials/Strategy and/or Techniques
AT PRESENT THE STUDENT IS PERFORMING AT LEVEL _____ IN THE REPRODUCTION OF SOUNDS.	TO INCREASE THE STUDENT'S PERFORMANCE IN REPRODUCING MUSIC SOUNDS TO A LEVEL OF _____	GIVEN A VARIETY OF ENVIRONMENTAL, VOCAL, AND INSTRUMENTAL MUSIC SOUNDS ADAPTED WHERE NECESSARY FOR THE HANDICAPPED STUDENT, THE STUDENT WILL REPRODUCE THESE SOUNDS AS PRESENTED BY THE TEACHER AT A LEVEL OF _____			Modality Strengths _____ Modality Weaknesses _____ MUSIC ELEMENTS TO BE REPRODUCED BY THE STUDENT (THOSE CIRCLED): SOUND/SILENCE LOUD/SOFT FAST/SLOW HIGH/LOW LONG/SHORT ACCENTED/ UNACCENTED EVEN/UNEVEN
LEVEL 1 0-20% accuracy					
LEVEL 2 20-40% accuracy					
LEVEL 3 40-60% accuracy					
LEVEL 4 60-80% accuracy					
LEVEL 5 80-100% accuracy					

Name _____   Teacher _____   Date _____

EACH AREA OF THE MULTIPLE CRITERIA LISTED MUST BE ADDRESSED: GENERAL HEALTH; MOTOR; LANGUAGE; VISUAL MOTOR; BEHAVIOR; SOCIAL/EMOTIONAL DEVELOPMENT; ACADEMIC ACHIEVEMENT.

Present Level of Performance	Annual Goals	Specific Instructional Objectives	Evaluation Criteria	Projected Date of Mastery	Materials/Strategy and/or Techniques
AT PRESENT THE STUDENT DEMONSTRATES A GENERAL KNOWLEDGE OF MUSIC AT A LEVEL OF ____. LEVEL 0 undetermined LEVEL 1 unsatisfactory LEVEL 2 fair LEVEL 3 satisfactory LEVEL 4 good LEVEL 5 superior	TO INCREASE THE STUDENT'S GENERAL KNOWLEDGE OF MUSIC TO A LEVEL OF ____.	GIVEN A LIST OF 12 SPECIAL PROJECTS ADAPTED FOR THE HANDICAPPED STUDENT, THE STUDENT WILL DEMONSTRATE HIS/HER KNOWLEDGE OF HISTORY, LITERATURE, COMPOSERS, MUSICIANS, AND INSTRUMENTS BY COMPLETING AT A LEVEL OF ____ ____ SPECIAL PROJECTS.			Modality Strengths Modality Weaknesses 1. REPORTS FEATURING COMPOSERS, PERFORMERS, INSTRUMENTS, AND COUNTRIES. 2. RADIO SHOWS 3. POSTERS 4. BULLETIN BOARDS 5. BUILDING INSTRUMENTS 6. TAKING INSTRUMENTS APART 7. FIELD TRIPS 8. INTEREST STATIONS 9. PERFORMING GROUPS 10. MUSIC GAMES 11. SONG WRITING 12. INSTRUMENTAL COMPOSITIONS

This form was prepared by Michael Rohrbacher, Registered Therapist, Baltimore (MD.) City Public Schools.

3 Guidelines for Mainstreaming in Music Education

WHAT IS MAINSTREAMING?

Public Law 94-142 stipulates that learning opportunities are to be provided to handicapped students in the "least restrictive environment commensurate with their needs." It is to this concept that the designation *mainstreaming* has been given. The concept means different things to different individuals. Music educators and others who plan individualized music programs and music for the handicapped should understand that though the basic and most important interpretation of this concept is that of education for the handicapped in regular music class situations, other alternatives are to be considered.

For some handicapped students, the "least restrictive" alternative may imply limited participation of some handicapped students with nonhandicapped students. For example, some students with physical or mental anomalies may be able to sing with the regular class but might need special music education and related services to learn the rhythms aspect of the music education curriculum. Furthermore, the "most appropriate" individual education program in music for some profoundly handicapped students might best take place in special, or "resource," rooms or in special institutions.

The overriding consideration, wherever the physical placement of the handicapped student, must be that the music-education experience become a factor in ending isolation of the student while at the same time providing academic, physical, social, and esthetic growth for the student. Since a fundamental consideration is the placement of the handicapped student in the regular music class whenever such placement is least restrictive, the following information will be directed toward the individualizing of music education, which is necessary to bring about such a procedure.

MAINSTREAMING IN THE REGULAR MUSIC CLASS

When a handicapped student has been properly assessed and placed, or mainstreamed, into a regular music class, it becomes the task of the music educator or classroom music teacher to personalize or individualize the music education of that student. This means that the music educator will teach toward obtaining the agreed-upon long-term (annual) goals in music in a manner that will emphasize the handicapped student's unique strength, style, and rate of learning, motivation, and talents as well as any difficulties that might be related to the handicapping condition. Specifically, the music educator will stress what can be done in the areas of singing, playing, listening and describing, moving, and creating. Concurrently, special personalized teaching methodologies will be employed along with adjustments in the content aspects of the music education curriculum to direct the child toward the already mentioned annual goals.

Here is an example. The class has been discussing the various modes of transportation in the world and has settled for the present upon the development of railroads in the United States. Some students bring model trains to class; others bring books, pictures, etc. One group works with the music educator to pursue these interests through music. The students also have some learning problems in reading. In the following pages suggestions incorporate music-education methodologies over a wide range of abilities for such a class.

MAINSTREAMING AND THE TEACHER

What does mainstreaming mean to the teacher? It means that the teacher will deal with students in the same manner in which good teachers have always dealt with students. The teacher will have a comprehensive understanding of the educational experiences needed for each student, will comprehend the goals of the educational program and have definitive knowledge of the objectives needed to reach the goals. The teacher will communicate the idea that learning is the focus and that everyone *can* learn.

The teacher will demonstrate mastery of good teaching techniques by

- Observing the response (or lack of response) of *each* student
- Trying many different approaches, using a variety of media and activities
- Commanding and holding the attention of a large group
- Organizing and monitoring small-group activity
- Identifying and often producing individualized learning packets

The teacher will nurture creativity, carefully setting the stage by fostering a respectful attitude in the classroom, encouraging each student's individual response, providing materials and equipment for exploration and experimentation, and urging students to "think of another way," asking them, "What would happen if . . . ?" Specific examples may be found in Chapter 4, Objectives C-2, C-3; D-4, D-6, D-7.

MAINSTREAMING AND SELF-CONCEPT

The following excerpt (Graham, 1975) summarizes the importance of music education for the exceptional student and the role of the teacher in providing music experiences:

Body Image and Self-concept

Basic to any process or progress in music education in the exceptional child is the development and preservation of accurate body image and healthy self-concept. Some subject disciplines in special education would explain the body image as a concept of self. Fortunately, intelligently arranged and developed music experiences from the earliest possible age lead to the concurrent development of body image and self-concept.

One means of further development is through the use, from an early age, of singing games, that make repeated reference to body parts and to the child's name such as, "Looby Loo," "Mulberry Bush." As the child develops and becomes more proficient in the performance of music, he learns to use his body in increasingly refined responses. Invariably, with developing musical abilities, comes an ever increasing awareness of both parts of the body, directly involved in music making, and later the entire body as it supports the directly concerned appendages of the vocal mechanism. In the course of developing an accurate image of his own and other's bodies, the child learns to interpret the meanings of his musical encounters with others. These encounters, including the reaction of the music educator—approval, disapproval, praise, criticism—are the bases for developing the healthy concept of self that is so essential to the adjustment of the exceptional child [pp. 10–11].

The following activity is suggested as one means of helping handicapped children improve their concept of self as they improve their music skills and increase their store of musical knowledge.

PROBLEM
Students with a poor self-concept in the regular classroom.

KEY IDEAS
Tailor the tasks to the students' ability level so that both teacher and students will *expect* success.

photo by Jack Engeman

Find areas of the students' behavior that deserve praise and then praise generously.

Insure success by moving forward slowly and in small steps.

Help the students learn how to make judgments.

AN EXAMPLE
Objective: The student will create a percussion piece, selecting one of four options.

The teacher will

- Teach (or review) a song having rhythmic patterns that are easily discernible. It is helpful if some are repeated. For example, "Are You Sleeping," page 47, has three patterns:

- Assign one type of instrument (or body sound) to play the rhythm of the melody (or words) of the song; assign a different type of instrument (or body sound) to play the underlying pulse. Combine the two sounds as the class sings the song.
- Play the accompaniment without singing aloud (think the tune or words).
- Ask students to suggest different instruments or body sounds for each pattern.
- Ask students to experiment with a different sequence of patterns —for example:

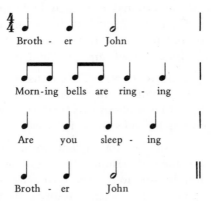

- Ask students to experiment with a constant repetition of one pattern (ostinato). For example, play this pattern repeatedly as an accompaniment:

Morn-ing bells are ring - ing.

- Review the three different methods of creating a percussion piece:
  1. Change the instruments.
  2. Change the sequence of patterns.
  3. Use one pattern as an ostinato.

- Ask students to choose one of the following options and create an original percussion piece:

  I will create a percussion piece by

  1. Changing the sequence of rhythm patterns found in "Are You Sleeping." I will select one type of instrument for a steady underlying pulse and a different instrument for the patterns.
  2. Changing the sequence of rhythm patterns found in a piece other than "Are You Sleeping," selecting one type of instrument for a steady underlying pulse and a different instrument for the patterns.
  3. Selecting a pattern to be used repeatedly throughout as an ostinato, and determining a sequence of three patterns. The ostinato and the three patterns will be taken from "Are You Sleeping" *or* "Go Down Moses."
  4. Devising an original ostinato and selecting at least two patterns from "Go Down Moses" to be arranged in a sequence of my choice and played on instruments of my choosing. The piece will include one soft and one loud part.

- It is important to go over the options very thoroughly so that all students are familiar with the choices available. It should also be pointed out that students may work in a group, or they may plan their piece independently to be played later by a group.

- Allow sufficient time for students to make a realistic choice, and then have them determine the length of time needed to fulfill the option. Be sure to have each composition played for the class. Insist upon absolute silence respectfully given as each piece is performed. Evaluate each composition in terms of fulfilling the terms of the option, not in terms of subjective judgments of bad or good.

NOTE

In this example the students' poor self-concept is dealt with by

Giving students an adequate background of experiences so that success is assured.

Providing a choice of activities on several levels of difficulty, making it possible for students to choose one in which they feel confident.

Designing the tasks in such a way that there is more than one "right" way to perform the tasks.

Evaluating the product in terms of objective data (Were the requirements met?) rather than subjective opinion of the quality (Was it good or bad?).

Are You Sleeping

Traditional

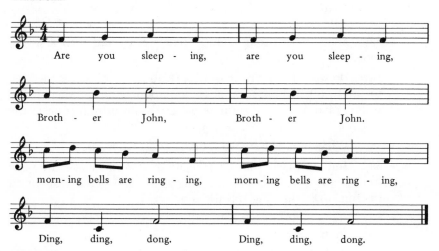

GENERAL PROBLEMS

Other problems that are dealt with in the following suggested activities include (1) span of attention, (2) general communication problems, and (3) multisensory needs.

SPAN OF ATTENTION

PROBLEM

A wide range of attention spans, some very short.

KEY IDEAS

> *Refrain* from too much "teacher talk"; count each word.
>
> *Pace* the lesson fast; move from one activity to the next with no dead time.
>
> *Plan* activity-centered lessons.
>
> *Develop* depth through constant repetition, using a variety of activities to master the same skill or concept.

AN EXAMPLE

Objective: Given a series of selected activities, the student will sing, "New River Train," page 49, pronouncing the words correctly and singing the melody and rhythm accurately.

The teacher will

- Say, "What is this song about?" (five words) and then sing the song.
- Say, "Do what I do." (Four words.) (Rub palms of hands together to produce a rubbing sound in imitation of train wheels. Try rubbing hands in an eight-note pattern as an introduction to the song.)
- Say, "What sounds were we imitating?" (Five words.)
- Say, "Imitate playing an instrument that would make the same sound." (Ten words.) Sing the song again, giving one student an instrument as the song is being sung.
- Say, "Stand and do what I do." (Perform simple body sounds; see music footnote, page 49.) (Six words.) Sing song again.
- Say, "Say the words and do the hand jive." (Eight words.) (See footnote.)
- Say, "Sing." (One word.)

NOTE

Special needs of students with short attention spans are attended to in the total group by

Employing many activities to teach one song.

Limiting verbal instructions.

Giving concise directions.

Modeling when possible.

Maintaining a constant flow of activities.

Including necessary repetition.

New River Train *

American Folk Song

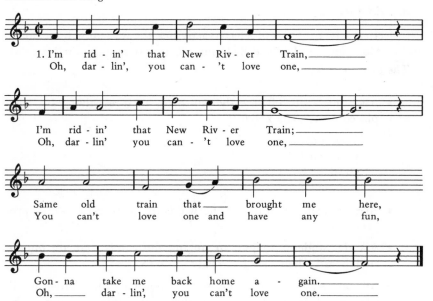

I'm ridin' that New River Train,_____
Oh, darlin', you can't love one,_____

I'm ridin' that New River Train;_____
Oh, darlin' you can't love one,_____

Same old train that_____ brought me here,
You can't love one and have any fun,

Gonna take me back home again._____
Oh,_____ darlin', you can't love one._____

GENERAL COMMUNICATION

PROBLEM

A wide range of reading levels.

---

* Accompanying hand jive:

"I'm ridin' that New River Train" *(Slap knees.)*
"I'm ridin' that New River Train" *(Clap.)*
"Same old train that brought me here," *(Snap fingers.)*
"Gonna take me back home again." *(Tap feet, alternating right and left.)*

The teacher may wish to change the motions, change the order, or ask students to lead.

KEY IDEAS

Use pictures and visual aids.

Select songs with few words and many repeated words.

Provide many opportunities for participation that do not require reading skills, such as playing an ostinato or a rhythm instrument or singing only a repeated phrase or the refrain.

Articulate the words of songs very well, using lips, tongue and teeth, facial expression, and gestures to aid learning the words.

AN EXAMPLE

Objective: Given a series of selected activities, the student will memorize and sing four stanzas of "She'll Be Comin' Round the Mountain," page 51.
The teacher will

- Ask students to observe the words (or pictures) that have been placed on the chalkboard:

   "Toot-toot"
   "Whoa-back"
   "Hi Babe"
   "Um-um"

- Sing the song, pointing to the words (or pictures) at the appropriate time.

- Ask the students to join in singing the words that are on the chalkboard when they feel ready to do so.

- Ask one student who reads well to point to the words on the chalkboard as the class acts out the words while listening to the song. Words are usually acted out as follows:

"Toot-toot" "Whoa-back"   "Hi babe"   "Um yum"

- Sing the song again, inviting students who are ready to sing those words to do so; all are invited to act out the words.
- Point to the words on the chalkboard and ask the students to say the phrase that follows each word.
- Repeat as needed.
- Invite students to sing as much of the song as they are able.
- Remove the words on the chalkboard one at a time when most students are able to sing the song.
- Ask students to sing the song without acting out the words.
- Ask students to sing the entire song from memory.

NOTE

Special needs are attended to in the regular class by

Asking students to sing when they are ready, so that no one is embarrassed.

Permitting better readers to assume a role of leadership.

Acting out the words, to aid memory.

Using visual aids.

She'll Be Comin' 'round the Mountain

Southern Folk Song

com- in' 'round the   moun-tain when she   comes.

2. She'll be drivin' six white horses when she comes,
   (Whoa, Back!) (Toot, Toot)
3. Oh, we'll all go out to meet her when she comes,
   (Hi, Babe!) (Whoa, Back!) (Toot, Toot)
4. Oh, we'll all have chicken and dumplings when she comes
   (Um—Um) (Hi Babe!) (Whoa Back!) (Toot, Toot).

PROBLEM

Students with special language needs in the regular class.

KEY IDEAS

Learn as much as possible about the students' level of language development and their needs.

Provide many concrete experiences and relate them to language.

Use every possible means of developing language in *every* music lesson.

AN EXAMPLE

Objective: The student will sing a song accurately by reading key words.
The teacher will

- Sing the first stanza of a song dealing with concrete things, such as "Hokey Pokey," page 53.

- Ask students what part of the body is mentioned in the song.

- Sing the song again, asking what action the song describes.

- Ask students to listen to the first stanza again and act out the words. (Observe students to see whether they understand "in," "out," "shake," "turn." If they do not, teach the word meaning immediately.)

- Write the word *foot* on the chalkboard or on a large card. Teach the word *foot*. (The words *right* and *left* could also be worked on.)

- Ask the class to sing the song and point to the word *foot* each time it occurs in the first verse.

- Repeat the procedure, having a student point to the word at the appropriate time.

- Follow the same procedure to teach the name of other parts of the body.

- Use the words (on cards or on the chalkboard) to change the order of the action by asking students to respond appropriately.

NOTE

In this example language development was enhanced by

Providing concrete experiences and then associating them with the written word (*foot, hand,* etc.).

Teaching words such as *in* and *out* through actual experience.

Providing a gamelike approach to learning.

The Hokey Pokey

American Play Party Song

1. You put your right foot in,— you take your right foot out,—
You put your right foot in— and shake it all a- bout,
And then you do the hok - ey pok - ey And you turn your-self a -
bout, And that's what it's all a - bout. HEY!

2. You put your left foot in,...
3. You put your right hand in,..
4. You put your left hand in,...
5. You put your right hip in,...
6. You put your left hip in,...
7. You put your whole self in,...

SENSORY NEEDS

PROBLEM

Students with a special need for multisensory approach (auditory, kinesthetic, and tactile) in a regular music class.

KEY IDEAS

Start (usually) with the auditory stimulus of music and then use visual, kinesthetic, and tactile stimuli.

Remember to incorporate appropriate auditory, visual, kinesthetic, and tactile stimuli in each lesson.

Observe students' responses and build on strengths.

AN EXAMPLE

Objective: The student will respond to music with some type of movement (see Objective D-1).

The teacher will

- Identify a space large enough for each student to move his or her arms in a very large arc.
- Strum a chord on the guitar, asking students to swing their arms (demonstrating an arc) as long as they can hear the sound, and then stop ("freeze").
- Ask some students to draw the arc, which represents the movement, on the chalkboard, "freezing" when the sound can no longer be heard.
- Ask some students to place one hand on the back of the guitar and trace the arc with the other hand, "freezing" when they can no longer feel the vibrations.
- Repeat until all students start and stop with the sound.
- Play a short chord progression and finally a longer composition, as the students continue to start and stop with the music, incorporating other types of movement.

NOTE

Special needs for auditory, visual, kinesthetic, and tactile stimulation are met in this example by

Tracing an arc in the air, using large muscles.

Observing or tracing the arc traced on the chalkboard.

Feeling the vibration of the guitar.

Hearing the music.

MAINSTREAMING REQUIRES INDIVIDUALIZED INSTRUCTION

The preceding music-education activities are designed to bring about music education of handicapped children in a regular classroom. It should be noted that no "labels" were used and that children were described more in terms of their learning styles than by their categories of exceptionality. This is in keeping with Public Law 94-142, which requires "specially designed instruction . . . to meet the unique needs of a handicapped child." The implications of this statement for music educators (and others) is that special education in music will take place not because a child is handicapped but because that child has educational needs which are peculiar to him or her and require specially designed music education. With this concept in mind, mainstreaming of handicapped children into regular music classes is accomplished through careful planning of music-learning experiences which facilitate progress for the handicapped individual in as many areas of the music curriculum as possible.

MAINSTREAMING STUDENTS WITH PARTICULAR HANDICAPS

The effort to write individualized education plans in response to learning problems is basic to successful mainstreaming in music classes. However, P. L. 94-142 does define the "handicapped children" for whom the Act was written. They are children who are "mentally retarded, hard-of-hearing, visually handicapped, seriously emotionally disturbed, or children with specific learning disabilities who by reason thereof require special education and related services." The following pages will touch upon some of the teaching strategies which might be employed to facilitate the mainstreaming of children with learning problems that one might logically expect to find associated with the following handicapping conditions.

THE MENTALLY RETARDED CHILD

Traditionally, the mentally retarded (mentally handicapped) have been grouped into three categories as a result of some one or combination of psychometric measurements: the mildly retarded, the severely retarded, and the profoundly retarded. The labels or diagnoses differ depending upon the setting and the professional discipline of the evaluator, but these three groupings have served the purposes of most mental retardation specialists for a good many years. When schools first started to experiment with mainstreaming in the 1960s and, in a few cases, earlier, it was primarily with the mildly retarded child in music or art classes. Apparently, many of the administrators thought then—and some still do—that the arts and (later) physical education did not require the same amount of "mental ability" as did the "basic academic courses."

There is no basis for such an assumption. In fact, there have been several studies which have strongly indicated a high correlation between measured intelligence and music abilities. On the other hand, there is no evidence whatsoever that advanced skills or knowledge in one or another of the academic subjects is a prerequisite for advanced skills or even knowledge in music and the other arts. There are numerous accounts of so-called mentally retarded children who sing, play, listen, move to, and create music—particularly the kind or style of music of their particular culture. On occasions when these children have been identified as mentally retarded by the music educator, it is because these children have not been successful at "classroom music," or have been unable to do reading assignments which related to the music being studied. Such identification would be due to inappropriate and biased evaluation and assessment. These same children assessed and instructed in the music of their cultures or subcultures might very well be seen to excel. In such instances, individualization and mainstreaming are directly related to relevancy of curriculum content. The task of the music educator is to plan a program that is meaningful and interesting to the child. Given even a mild interest in music, with proper leadership from the music educator or classroom teacher, the mildly mentally retarded child can be effectively educated in the regular music class.

Some suggestions for working with the mildly retarded child in the regular class follow:

1. Begin the music-education program at the earliest possible age; a preschool music-education program is highly advisable.

2. Provide a good singing model for the child at an early age and encourage the child to, first, copy the singing model, and, second, sing along with the singing model.

3. Demonstrate the posture and other behaviors associated with good listening habits. Reinforce approximations of these behaviors whenever they occur at early ages.

4. Encourage the child to experiment with the singing voice and with other sound sources within the context of the regular music class. Special singing and instrumental activities will have to be developed by the music educator to facilitate such activities.

5. Make certain that every "reading song" has been thoroughly learned by rote before any attempt is made to read the song from the printed page.

6. Provide opportunities for the mentally retarded child to exhibit his music skills frequently in the regular music class setting.

7. Permit the child to have some leadership experiences in the areas of his personal music strength.

8. Even when slow cognitive development prevents high levels of music functioning, arrange music experiences which will permit group participation by the handicapped child (e.g., singing simplified parts in vocal ensembles, playing one rather than a variety of classroom instruments, thus permitting the development of at least one reliable skill).

9. Encourage the child to practice weak areas at home under the direction of the parents or other interested persons with at least some rudimentary knowledge of the music skills being practiced.

10. Never base progress in music solely on the basis of acquisition of one skill or another (particularly not upon music-reading skills). Music is by nature multifaceted and permits progress of the individual in many ways.

PROBLEM

A wide range of rates of learning in the regular class.

KEY IDEAS

Vary the amount of practice or worktime to suit individual needs.

photo by Jack Engeman

Individualize or subgroup practice or work time.

Vary the difficulty of the assignments.

Give home assignments when appropriate.

AN EXAMPLE

Objective: Given a series of selected activities, the student will play one of three bell parts as an accompaniment to a song. The part will be played accurately in pitch and rhythm.

The teacher will

- Teach the class the song, "Two Wings," page 60.

- Call attention to the octave leap found over the words "want two" each time they occur. Identify the two C's on melody bells.

- Identify a student to play the two C's appropriately as the class sings the song. Prepare a visual aid such as

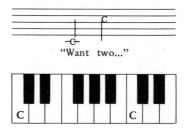

"Want two..."

- Teach the class to sing the first four tones of the song from low G to C as

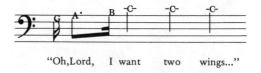

"Oh, Lord,   I want   two   wings..."

- Identify a student to play those tones on the resonator bells, metalaphone, or xylophone. Prepare a visual aid so that the student can work independently, such as

- Explain how the bass bell part can be read by referring to the chart below:

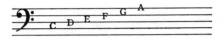

- Ask the class to clap a half-note pattern as the song is sung again, pointing to the bass bell part that is written entirely in half notes as

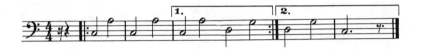

- Assign each student a part to practice that is appropriate to his rate of learning. (If there are not sufficient instruments for each student, assign two students to each instrument. Some classes can function very well when as many as five students are assigned to each instrument. If there is a piano in the room, be sure to use it, too.)
- Ask students to play the parts that have been mastered as an accompaniment to the singing. (Some students may need more practice time, which can be a before-school, noontime, or after-school activity.)

NOTE

Special needs of students with different rates of learning are met in the total group by

Giving assignments of varying difficulty.

Knowing the rate of learning of the students.

Allowing practice periods of different lengths of time.

Spending part of the class time in individual or small-group work.*

Giving adequate preparation so that each student can be successful.

* Detailed suggestions for individual and small group instruction may be found in Beer and Hoffman, *Teaching Music What, How, Why* (Morristown, N.J.: General Learning Press, 1973), pp. 83–115.

Two Wings

Spiritual

From *Expressing Music* New Dimensions Series, American Book Co. © by Litton Educational Publishing, Inc.

THE HEARING-IMPAIRED STUDENT

The trend toward mainstreaming deaf and hard-of-hearing students was well underway in the mid-1960s. Unfortunately, there were too many instances of these children's being kept out of music classes, usually in favor of art classes to meet the "fine arts requirement" for the high school diploma. It is the position of the authors that such a practice is unsound educationally and discriminatory against the hearing-impaired.

Most hearing-impaired students do have some hearing. Where the hearing loss is only mild or moderate, the child should be given every opportunity to use whatever residual hearing is available in regular music-education classes. It is up to the teacher to be particularly aware of good classroom procedures which should be followed in all situations: speaking clearly and loudly enough to be heard throughout the room, and checking often with the class to be certain that instructions are clearly understood. When good classroom procedures are followed, hearing-impaired students with impairments to the moderately severe level (56- to 70-decibel loss) can participate in singing, playing, listening, moving, and creative experiences with normal students. The students may even excel in rhythmic activities.

The totally deaf student will have considerable difficulty in learning to produce melody and the most difficulty in the area of harmony. This is not to suggest that the few totally deaf students who might be mainstreamed into the regular music class should not participate in melodic and harmonic experiences. What is called for is specialized assistance by the deaf-education specialists and extensive use of singing and pitch–muscle training. The combination of certain muscle tensions and certain pitch levels provides a means of teaching even the totally deaf to produce reasonable intonation in singing and playing certain musical instruments.

For all hearing-impaired students, experiences in movement to music are of particular importance to their overall development: physical, language, and esthetic. From movement experiences to rhythmic pulses the student is able to learn something of sequencing, rhythmic pacing, repetition, contrast, and so forth. These concepts are essential to the development of language as well as to the development of music responsiveness. Drum techniques have proven to be an effective means of developing these concepts in the hearing-impaired student in the regular music class.

On the subject of integrating or mainstreaming the hearing-impaired student into the regular classroom Bruce (1973) wrote:

> Integrated educational settings for the hearing-impaired range from those that offer mere physical proximity with hearing pupils to those in which the hearing-impaired children are completely independent of supportive personnel. A child may be integrated as early as 0–3 years or as late as high school age. The effective implementation of integration is dependent on the quality of personnel, equipment, transportation, and curriculum [p. 213].

Reynolds and Birch (1977) add:

> The curriculum that needs the most adaptation for hearing-impaired pupils is obviously that which depends on accurate hearing. Music is a concrete example. But there is no curriculum content hearing impaired pupils cannot learn in a meaningful way [p. 561].

There are increasing accounts in the literature of music education and elsewhere of music educators who have included hearing impaired pupils in their regular classes. Some of the suggestions for music educators from that literature are as follows:

1. Seat the student as near as possible to the music educator and the sound source. Make certain that the student can see the teacher's speech movements.
2. Music sounds will be made louder by hearing aids, but there may be some sound distortion in the higher and lower pitch

ranges. This distortion should be discussed with the student for clarification and explanation.

3. When explaining the handling of musical instruments, it is advisable to hold the instrument and demonstrate any verbal explanations.

4. Students will have to turn down the hearing aids during group singing or playing. Everything is made louder by the hearing aid, and the optimal level for loudness will have to be found by experimentation during group music efforts.

5. The large majority of hearing-impaired students have some hearing. They can hear some music and can be taught to appreciate it as an important part of their lives.

Following are some suggestions for music students in selected music activities.

PROBLEM

A few hearing-impaired students in the regular class.

KEY IDEAS

Learn as much as possible about each student: the degree of impairment, any uniqueness in speech, the need for reinforcement in speech improvement, the ability to speech-read, etc.

photo by Jack Engeman

Ask a responsible student to sit next to the hearing-impaired student to give assistance as needed.

Remember the importance of distinct articulation.

Use many visual aids, including objects, pictures, the chalkboard, gestures, facial expression, etc.

photo by Jack Engeman

Seat the hearing-impaired student where he or she can hear as much as possible and see everything easily.

Make use of the sound vibrations of music. Use hard wooden surfaces to transmit vibrations of drums, other instruments, and recordings.

photo by Jack Engeman

AN EXAMPLE

Objective: Given a series of selected activities, the student will play a repeated pattern, first on a drum and then on a melody instrument (see Objective C-4, page 121).

The teacher will

- Teach the class to sing a song with a repeated pattern that is easily identifiable, such as the pattern of

found in the song "Sweet Potato," page 65.

- Teach the class to sing the song very well.
- Placing a large drum (conga) on the floor, play the pattern on the drum:

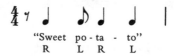

- Ask the class to sing the song, playing the pattern each time it occurs. (Be sure that the hearing-impaired student is near the drum.)
- Ask a volunteer to play the drum part as the class sings the song again.
- Point to the words "Sweet potato" each time they occur in the song. (Have the words written on a chart or the chalkboard and tap the rhythm of the words each time.)
- Play the same pattern on the C octave:

(It may help to tap the foot on the eighth-beat rest.)

- Ask the class to sing.
- Ask a volunteer to play the octave pattern as the class sings the song. (If the class is advanced, the pattern can be sung throughout the song.)

Sweet Potato

Louisiana Folk Song
Adapted by Nancy Forbes

2. Now it's done, but don't burn your fingers,
   Watch your fingers, watch your fingers!
   Now it's done, but don't burn your fingers,
   It is mighty hot!
3. Add a heap of good yellow butter,
   Yellow butter, yellow butter,
   Add a heap of good yellow butter,
   I can eat a lot!

NOTE

Special needs of the hearing-impaired students in the regular class are met in the total group by

Using the drum to transmit vibrations.
Employing the chart (or chalkboard) as a visual aid.
Modeling the activities.

THE ORTHOPEDICALLY HANDICAPPED
OR OTHER HEALTH-IMPAIRED STUDENT

Mainstreaming of the orthopedically handicapped and other health-impaired had started considerably before the writing of Public Law 94-142. The Act will, it is hoped, aid in the continued smooth integration of such students into regular classes, including regular music-education classes. The music educator has the job of coordinating his or her efforts with those of special therapists and medical specialists for the best possible music education of the physically handicapped and health-impaired student.

The initial assessment in music should be accomplished jointly with the assistance of the student's corrective therapists. Varying degrees and styles of physical mobility will require that considerable latitude be given in accessing certain areas of student performance. For example, substitute or alternative measurements may have to be obtained for evaluation of the student's abilities in executing the "movement vocabulary" in music education (e.g., swinging, bending, stretching, walking, and so forth). This area of music education will have to be assessed in a nondiscriminatory manner so as to determine the child's true ability to respond bodily to music.

Music education of the physically handicapped or other health-impaired child may have to include use of crutches, braces, canes, wheelchairs, and appendage prostheses. Some music education may have to take place with the use of standing tables, page turners, and protective helmets. Rythm-and-movement activities could well require the use of special-purpose ramps, parallel bars, and handrails.

Often the music educator is called upon to design music and movement activities to supplement the physical therapy of some orthopedically impaired students. Generally, the student is in some transitory state toward independent locomotion. That is, if the child is presently able to participate in classroom activities only from the prone position, he might be working toward being able to operate from a sitting position—probably in a wheelchair. If he is able to function musically only from the wheelchair, it is likely that some orthopedic specialist is working with the child in the three-point-crutch stand. The child who can walk only with crutches is probably learning to walk without any support.

Music and movement activities are of twofold importance when they complement the physical therapy program designed to bring about greater mobility and, thus, greater freedom for the physically or health-impaired student. It is worth emphasizing once again that such programs should be developed only with the assistance of a bona fide health specialist.

In mainstreaming the health- or physically-impaired child, it is frequently necessary to prepare the remainder of the class for the entrance of such a child. A lecture or demonstration of the use of braces, crutches, and wheelchairs is suggested. The assignment of one or two students to assist the impaired student to various places in the room for his music education is helpful. It is also beneficial to all concerned when the class members can have a part in designing the music curriculum for the impaired child. This is part of the group effort that is so frequently desirable in music education.

THE SPEECH-IMPAIRED CHILD

The most common exceptionality in the United States is that of speech impairment. Though the great majority of speech problems are developmental and thus very amenable clinical or "correction" methodologies, some problems will call for medical treatment. Music educators will see very few cases of speech problems which call for medical treatment. On the other hand, music educators will see a considerable number of children who have the following disorders: stuttering, voice-quality disorders, delayed speech and language, and articulation problems. Of these, articulation defects are the most common, and the music educator, as well as all other teachers who come in contact with the child, is obliged to support the work of the speech specialist. This kind of support can be offered in the regular class by following a few simple suggestions and by designing the singing curriculum, particularly, to deal with the following articulation problems:

1. *Substitutions:* The student substitutes one sound for another such as "Huwah" for "Hurrah," or "Ober de wibuh and thwooh de wood" for "Over the river and through the wood."
2. *Omissions:* The student will omit some sounds such as " 'hen 'ohnny come' ma'ch'n 'ome 'gin" for "When Johnny comes marching home again."
3. *Distortions:* Some sounds are distorted, such as "Johnny Safto went to Schee" for "Johnny Shafto went to Sea."

The above types of speech errors can be helped considerably by the speech correctionists. Any effort to assist in alleviating these problems must be thoroughly worked out with the speech clinician, and it is also advisable that some indication be made in the IEP of support efforts by the music educator.

Some suggestions for support of speech correction in singing:

1. Use songs as speech-stimulus experiences. Select songs which are accompanied by pictures (the typical elementary songbooks are

excellent sources). Make every effort to have all sounds represented in initial, medial, and final position.

2. Use the tape recorder frequently. Take examples of students singing and speaking the same words.

3. Work with a speech clinician to incorporate developmental sound schedules into class songs. Develop a series of songs that incorporate sounds in the order that most children learn them.

4. Take inservice course work in speech correction to facilitate working with the speech clinician.

The following music activities are designed for the music educator or classroom teacher to use in support of the speech correction programs designed by a certified speech clinician.

PROBLEM

A few students with speech problems in the regular class.

KEY IDEAS

Learn as much as possible about the nature of the problem, conferring with the speech therapist.

Seat the student with speech problems in a position where he or she is surrounded by students with good speech.

Listen for speech problems and errors.

Make certain that the student hears speech errors.

Assist the student in making the correct sound (without embarrassment, of course).

Model good speech in both speaking and singing at all times.

AN EXAMPLE

Objective: Given a series of selected activities, the student will sing a song, articulating each syllable, consonant, and vowel clearly (see Objective A-5, page 99).

The teacher will

- Select an attractive song with a reasonable number of words and some repetition, such as "When Johnny Comes Marching Home," page 69.

- Ask the students to listen to the song and think of some words that would describe the mood of the song. (Be sure to sing the words very distinctly.)

- Ask students to identify exact words in the song that helped them make their choices.

- Explain the importance of singing the words of any song distinctly so that listeners can interpret the song's mood and meaning.

- Sing the song a second time, asking the students to determine the exact order of events described in the song.

- Repeat the song until all events are recalled in the correct order. (It will help to list key words on the chalkboard as the events are recalled. In upper-level classes ask students to name action words, nouns, etc., and list them.)

- Teach the two short phrases that contain only the word "Hurrah."

- Sing the entire song, asking the students to sing only the two short phrases.

- Ask students to sing the entire song.

- Listen for words or phrases in which vowels or consonants are mispronounced; chant the words that are mispronounced or carelessly articulated.

- Listen for syllables that are omitted or added; chant the words and clap each syllable.

- Ask students to sing the song, remembering to sing the words clearly.

NOTE

Special needs of students having speech problems are attended to in the total group by

> *Listening* for speech errors in students' singing and speaking.
> *Making* certain that students are aware of the errors.
> *Correcting* errors by chanting words and clapping syllables.
> *Presenting* a model of good speech in speaking and singing.

When Johnny Comes Marching Home

Louis Lambert

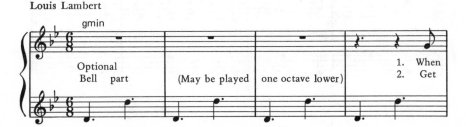

THE VISUALLY IMPAIRED CHILD

The visually impaired child presents very few problems in mainstreaming into the regular music class. For a good many years partially sighted and blind children have sung in school choruses and played in school instrumental ensembles. With the help of teachers who are certified for instruction of the visually impaired, the student can learn Braille music reading. The Braille music-writing machine (typewriter) or the stylus and slate can be used by the music educator after only a little practice to provide written music for the severely impaired child. The Braille music scheme is illustrated on page 72.

Some suggestions for teaching one or more visually impaired children in the regular music class follow.

PROBLEM

A few visually impaired students in the regular class.

KEY IDEAS

Adapt material by typing the words of songs on typewriters having large type (such a typewriter can be requested on the student's IEP) or by printing the words in large letters.

Use large letters when writing on the chalkboard.

Investigate the use of music printed in Braille.

Adapt equipment—for example, label Autoharp chords and resonator bell bars with large, easily read letters.

Give instructions orally. The visually impaired student will not know when the teacher is pointing or using any visual means of communication unless it is accompanied by an oral one.

Permit the visually impaired student to choose a seat so that he or she can see the chalkboard or movie screen.

Be sure to orient the visually impaired student to any change in room arrangement or placement of equipment.

Learn as much as possible about the student and whether there is need of a "buddy" to assist the student.

AN EXAMPLE

Objective: Given a series of selected activities, the student will play an accompaniment on the Autoharp using at least three chords (see Objective C-4, page 121).

Chart of Single Cell Braille Symbols
with Associated Meanings for Braille Music Notation

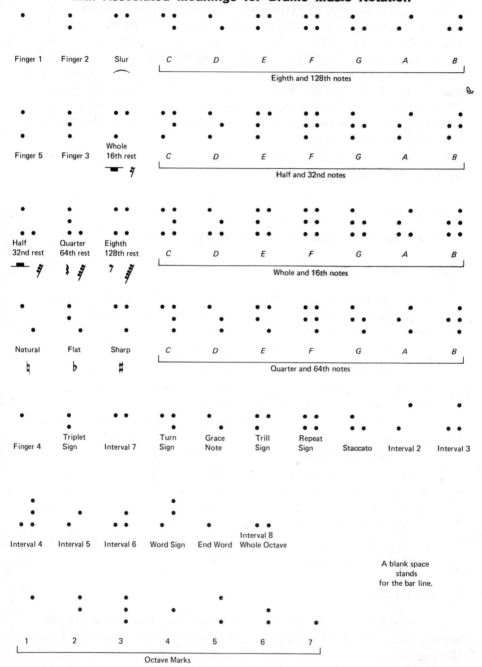

*Many multiple cell signs are also used in braille music notation.

The teacher will

- Label the F, C⁷ B♭ chords on an Autoharp by writing the letters as large as possible, using a black felt-tipped pen on a white label.

- Select a song requiring no more than three chords, such as "One More River," page 74.

- Teach the song to the class, using an Autoharp accompaniment.

- Play the Autoharp accompaniment without singing, asking the students to show with some movement (clap, raise hands, stand, etc.) each time they hear a chord change. (Be sure to situate the Autoharp outside the range of vision of students so that they will be required to hear rather than see the changes.)

- Repeat the activity, singing the song along with the accompaniment.

- Demonstrate how the fingers are placed on the keys of the Autoharp to play the F and C⁷ chords, asking students to imitate the position. (Traditionally the chord buttons are pushed with the left hand; consequently, the demonstration should be done by facing the front of the room and extending the two fingers to be used high in the air so that everyone can see.)

- Write a large F and C⁷ on the chalkboard in the same position they are found on the Autoharp:

- Ask the class to sing the song and indicate chord changes by pointing to the correct letter name and using the correct finger.

- Remind the students that the first chord is F and that the change occurs on the word "cross." Sing and ask students to practice pointing with the correct finger on the verse only. (This can be done on the desk or pantomimed in the air.)

- Identify a student who has mastered the chord change and ask him or her to play the Autoharp accompaniment as the class sings.

- Provide for many students to play the Autoharp on the verse.

- Follow the same procedure for teaching the chords used in the refrain.

NOTE

Special needs of the visually impaired student are met in this example by

> *Insisting* that all students recognize chord changes by ear rather than by eye.
>
> *Adapting* an instrument so that the visually impaired student can see the chord names.
>
> *Writing* large letters on the chalkboard.
>
> *Providing* for a responsible "buddy" as needed.
>
> *Telling* the students where the chord changes occur in addition to pointing to them.

One More River

Spiritual

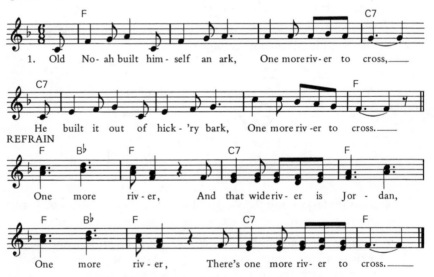

2. The animals came two by two, One more river to cross,
   The elephants and kangaroo, One more river to cross.
3. The animals came three by three, one more river to cross,
   The baboon and the chimpanzee, One more river to cross.
4. The animals came four by four, One more river to cross,
   The hippopotamus got stuck in the door, One more river to cross.
5. The animals came five by five, One more river to cross,
   The bees came swarming from the hive, One more river to cross.

THE SEVERELY EMOTIONALLY
DISTURBED CHILD

The severely emotionally disturbed student perhaps offers the most serious challenge to the music educator. The nature of the music class is that of heightened emotions or symbolic enactment of emotional states. Students sing of happiness, sorrow, patriotism, love, loss, death, religion, and so forth. There is a difficulty inherent in the effort to encourage children to express emotion on the one hand and yet to control emotion on the other. As in the case of other children with other handicapping conditions, this is not to suggest that emotionally disturbed children should not participate in music activities. On the contrary, there are many documented occasions of emotionally disturbed children's finding their most meaningful emotional expressions through expressive and well-executed music experiences.

Whatever the approach to curriculum and program planning in music, the efforts of the music educator should be coordinated with those of a mental health specialist. The music educator should be instructed as to the extent of academic requirements, rule enforcement, unstructured activity, and independent work. With such parameters clearly established, the music curriculum for the emotionally disturbed student should proceed as much as possible in the same manner as the regular class.

The music educator should take every opportunity to label feelings and emotions expressed in songs and instrumental music. Appropriate social and physical response to music of various ceremonial occasions should be demonstrated. For example, the child should understand the expected social response to funeral music and how such responses differ from those to party music or martial music. Activities in which students simulate these experiences to the actual music used permit the kind of learning experience which is consistent with systematic behavior training of emotionally disturbed children.

When low tolerance for frustration appears to be a factor in the behavior of the seriously emotionally disturbed student, there are some basic steps in curriculum construction and classroom that the music educator should follow. Suggestions for such procedures are listed below.

PROBLEM

Students with an unusually low tolerance for frustration in the regular music class.

KEY IDEAS

Learn as much as possible about the students. Try to find the causes of their frustration.

Eliminate failure by organizing materials and methods.

Provide immediate feedback so that correct responses can be immediately reinforced.

Find the level at which the student is successful but challenged.

Provide many opportunities for repetition, using a variety of approaches.

photo by Jack Engeman

Provide for group experiences that make possible shared success.

AN EXAMPLE

Objective: The student will memorize two stanzas of a song, singing the song with good diction and accurate rhythm and pitch.

The teacher will

- Select a song with a phrase or pattern that occurs more than once, such as "Go Down Moses," page 78.

- Ask students to listen to the song to discover what they believe to be the main idea of the song.

- Sing the phrase "Let my people go" in isolation, and then ask students to count the number of times that phrase is heard in the song.

- Sing the first verse and the refrain again.

- Teach the phrase, repeating as many times as needed. (To make the activity interesting, add a finger-snapping accompaniment and repeat the phrase *in rhythm. Without breaking the rhythm* signal, first one group and then another group should sing the phrase alone.)

- Sing the entire song, asking students to sing only the repeated phrase.

- Ask students to listen to the words of the song, explaining that the words tell a story. Ask the students to find who the main characters are. (Be sure that students sing the repeated phrase.)

- Clarify word meanings, stressing correct pronunciation and enunciation.

- Ask students to listen again to find what action the main characters took. (Again, ask students to sing the repeated phrase.)

- Clarify word meanings, as needed.

- Ask students to sing the refrain and repeated phrase.

- Identify students who are able to sing the entire song, and ask others to sing only the refrain and repeated phrases.

- Ask entire class to sing the song.

- Work on places that are inaccurate or places where words are poorly articulated. (Use finger-snapping accompaniment as indicated above to make repetition more attractive.)

- Ask class to sing the entire song accurately and with good diction.

NOTE

Needs of students having low tolerance for frustration are met in this example by

Eliminating failure by working on small portions of the song at one time.

Providing immediate feedback on correct and incorrect responses of each small part of the song.

Providing for much repetition.

Providing a range of activities to meet individual levels of ability.

Providing a group experience that makes possible shared success.

Go Down Moses

Spiritual

1. When   Is - rael was in   E - gypt's land
   bold Moses said,   Let my peo-ple   go..."
2. "Thus   spoke the Lord",   bold Moses said,   Let my peo-ple   go..."

Op - pressed so   hard they   could not   stand,
   "Let my peo-ple   go."
"If   not   I'll   smite your   first born dead."   Let my peo-ple   go."

REFRAIN

Go   down,   Mo - ses,   "Way   down   in   E - gypt land,——

Tell__ old   Phar - aoh,   "Let my   peo- ple   go."

PROBLEM

A few students with emotional problems in the regular music class.

KEY IDEAS

Establish limits of behavior (with student input) that are clearly defined and consistently adhered to.

Stop inappropriate behavior as soon as it starts.

Plan a variety of activities, maintaining a balance between physical activity, playing, singing, and listening.

Be generous in making positive comments when they are earned.

Find a means by which a troubled student can be out of the room, or in a quiet place, if needed.

Make clear exactly what the task is and how it is to be completed.

Plan transitions from one activity to another carefully so that they can be accomplished in an orderly fashion.

Provide for success by selecting materials and planning activities that meet the ability and interest levels of the students.

AN EXAMPLE

Objective: The student will read and play (using drumsticks or rhythm instruments) quarter notes and eighth notes as an accompaniment to a selected piece of music.

The teacher will

- Review quarter-note and eighth-note values by clapping a short drill—for example:

- Praise those who earn it.
- If necessary, extend the drill by using echo clapping, finger snapping, foot tapping, knee slapping, or saying "ta, ta, ti, ti, ta, 1, 2, 1 and 2," etc.
- Clarify and review rules for handling the drumsticks or rhythm instruments (play position, rest position, and consequences for not abiding by the rules).
- Ask group leaders to take the container of drumsticks or instruments marked with their group's number and give each member a pair of drumsticks or an instrument.
- Praise leaders who earn it.
- Remind the class that instruments are to be placed in rest position.
- Demonstrate and review play position.
- Give a clear and concrete direction for play position.
- Praise those who deserve it.
- Start the record player, having selected a popular piece or a march in a moderate tempo.
- Indicate the quarter-note beat by clapping and then pointing to the notes in the drill, tapping the rhythm audibly so that all hear and understand the relationship between quarters and eighths.
- Give a clear direction for playing—for example, "Ready, play."

- Praise those who succeed.
- Give a clear direction for placing the sticks in rest position—for example, "Rest position."
- Give a concise direction for group leaders to return sticks or instruments to the appropriate container.
- Praise groups who earn it.

NOTE

In this example the teacher cares for the needs of students with emotional problems by

Reviewing the established limits of behavior in handling drumsticks or instruments.

Planning a variety of activities, varying them in mood and manual involvement.

Giving positive comments generously.

Making clear what the task is and when it is completed.

Planning transition from one activity to another so that the transition is orderly.

THE STUDENT WITH SPECIFIC LEARNING DISABILITIES

The United States Congress has defined children with specific learning disabilities in Public Law 94-142 as follows:

Those children who have a disorder in one or more of the basic psychological processes involved in understanding or in using language, spoken or written, which disorder may manifest itself in imperfect ability to listen, think, speak, read, write, spell or do mathematical calculations. Such disorders include such conditions as perceptual handicaps, brain injury, minimal brain dysfunction, dyslexia, and developmental aphasia. Such term does not include children who have learning problems which are primarily the result of visual, hearing or motor handicaps, of mental retardation, of emotional disturbance, or environmental, cultural or economic disadvantage [Section 5(B)4].

The combination of extreme detail and general inclusiveness of this description may lead music educators (and others) to assume either that no learning-disabled child would have difficulty in learning music or that all learning-disabled children would have difficulty.

The position of the authors of this book is that any combinations of characteristics or discrepencies in learning are less important than how music is taught to the student with specific learning disabilities. With fewer than ten years of dealing with children classified in this manner, the best answer appears to be that a high level of creative individualized music education is the best approach to children who appear to learn less efficiently in the regular classroom. The learning problems seem rarely to be associated with actual sound production. The child with learning disabilities can be expected to develop singing abilities at the rate of his peers in the regular class room. There is some reason to suspect that some of the manipulative skills associated with playing musical instruments might lag in development. Obviously, if a child is having difficulty in reading, his music-reading progress will be somewhat slowed. If numbers are a problem, it is likely that there will be some problem in sequencing or counting in rhythms and in music reading. Whatever the nature of the child's apparent difficulty, it should be viewed as a teacher problem at least as much as a student problem. It is for this reason that the authors take the position that any music problem which might ostensibly be related to a specific learning disability can be solved by a high quality of individualized instruction in the music class.

The following activities are offered as examples of how certain specific learning areas might be approached in the music education classroom containing children with specific learning disabilities.

PROBLEM

Students with a special need for kinesthetic and tactile learning experiences in a regular classroom.

KEY IDEAS

Respond to the elements of music through movement.

Trace pitch changes on the chalkboard or in the air.

Start (usually) with the aural stimulus of music and then use kinesthetic and tactile stimuli to reinforce the learning.

AN EXAMPLE

Objective: Given a series of selected activities, the student will identify, sing, and play an octave leap as it occurs in a song.

The teacher will

- Select a song with at least one easily identified octave leap, such as "Bye 'M Bye," page 83.

- Sing the song for the students, asking them to listen to the words and identify the ones that are repeated many times.

- Establish the connection between the repeated words and a lullaby.

- Ask the students what is being counted.

- Sing the song again, asking students to observe and follow hand motion on the words "Oh, my" (hand in high position for "Oh" and low position for "my," representing the octave leap).

- Place the two C resonator bells on a set of steps and play the octave leap. (Be sure to have the high C on the student's right.)

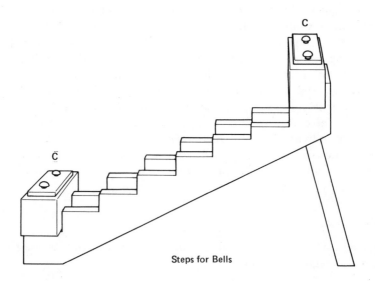

Steps for Bells

- Sing the song asking the students to pretend that they have two resonator bells and to play them on the words "Oh, my!" (Be sure that all play from right to left—that is, from high to low.)

- Ask the class to sing the song as a volunteer plays the two C's.

- Ask one or two students to trace the octave leap on the chalk-board as the class sings ( ).
- Ask the students which resonator bell is smaller, the high one or the low one.
- Place the two bells in a bag, and ask a student to extract the high bell by feeling the two bells.
- Reward the student by having him or her play the octave leap as the class sings.
- Place the two bells under a cover, asking a student to remove the high bell and place it on the proper step (high).
- Reward the student by having him or her play the octave as the class sings.
- Ask students to stand tall on the high C and squat on the low C. (This can be a class activity as one or two are selecting and arranging the bells.)

NOTE

Special needs of students for kinesthetic and tactile learning experiences were met in this example by

Tracing the pitch pattern of the octave leap in the air.
Pantomiming playing the resonator bells.
Tracing the pitch pattern of the octave leap on the chalkboard.
Identifying the high and low bells by feel.
Arranging the high and low bells by feel.
Responding to the octave leap through physical activity.

Bye 'M Bye

PROBLEM

Several visual learners in a regular music class.

KEY IDEAS

Learn as much as possible about the student so as to reinforce skill development.

Use all kinds of visual aids, including yourself, pictures, objects, visual representations, etc.

Observe the visual learners and be aware of their responses.

AN EXAMPLE

Objective: The student will identify like and unlike phrases in a song (see Objective A-5, page 99) and play them on bells (see Objective C-4, page 121).

The teacher will

- Select a song with phrases that are easily identified, such as "Hush-a-by," page 85, and make a visual representation of the song, such as

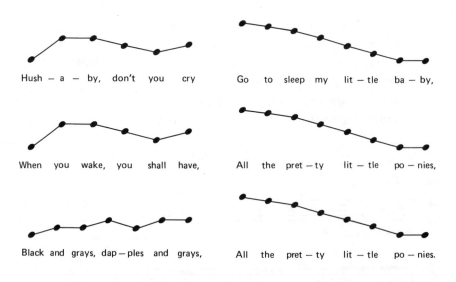

- Sing the song, simultaneously pointing to the visual representation of the melody, asking the students to listen and observe the chart to find phrases that are alike.

$$\frac{4}{4} \;\; \downarrow \;\; | \; \downarrow. \;\; \downarrow \; \downarrow \; \downarrow \;\; | \; \downarrow. \;\; \downarrow \; \downarrow$$

Oh   beau - ti - ful   for   spa - cious skies,

asking the class to respond by snapping their fingers on the second half of the phrase.

- Ask the students to substitute a percussion instrument for the clapping and a different instrument for the finger snapping. *Example:* Use tone block for first half and triangle for second half.
- Continue the process for the four phrases. *Example:*

Phrase 1:

Tone block and triangle

Phrase 2:

Tambourine and rhythm sticks

Phrase 3:

High drum and low drum

Phrase 4:

Tone block ⎫   ⎧ Triangle
Tambourine ⎬ and ⎨ Rhythm sticks
High drum ⎭   ⎩ Low Drum

- Encourage students to experiment with their choices until they achieve a sound that pleases them.
- Ask the class to think of a way in which their arrangement could be written so that another group could play it. *Example:*

All — — — — — — — — — —

All — — — — — — —

Or

1. Tone Block

2. Triangle

3. Tambourine

4. Rhythm Sticks

etc.

NOTE

Special needs of the auditory learner are met in this example by

Giving instructions orally.

Providing opportunities to suggest sounds to be used in creative work.

Encouraging students to symbolize sounds.

America The Beautiful

Words by Katherine Lee Bates
Music by Samuel Ward

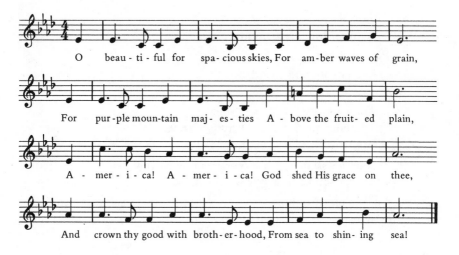

PROBLEM

Varying degrees of motor coordination among the students.

KEY IDEAS

Provide activities that require various degrees of motor coordination.

Allow ample time for practice where needed.

Separate practice on motor skills from other skills such as reading and listening.

AN EXAMPLE

Objective: The student will play a melody bell part as the class sings a song.

The teacher will

- Select a song with a melody that can be simplified, such as "Down the River," page 89.
- Teach the song.
- Ask students to respond to the accented first beat of each measure with some large-muscle activity (such as simulating rowing a boat). The accents fall on these words:
  "Down, down, down, go:
  Down, down, down, O."
- Ask students to observe the four bars on the melody bells (or resonator bells or metalaphone, etc.)—F, G, A, and B♭—noting how close together they are.
- Ask students to pretend that there is a set of bars on their desks and to play the four bars that are next to one another. (Practice until most students are pantomiming realistically. It will help if students sing the letter or syllable names as they pantomime.)
- Ask one or more student(s) to play the part on the bells. (Be sure that they play the part slowly.)
- Sing the song as the student plays the simplified part.
- Identify one or more students to play the entire melody as a few students play the simplified part.

NOTE

Varying degrees of motor coordination among students are dealt with in this example by

Providing for large-muscle activity.
Providing for small-muscle activity, both simple and complex.
Proceeding through a step-by-step progression, giving preparation for each new step.

Down The River

American River Song

Down   the   riv - er,   Oh,   down   the   riv - er,   Oh,

down the riv - er   we   go - o - o: Down   the   riv - er,   oh,

down   the   riv - er,   Oh,   down   the   O - hi - o!_____

Simplified Bell Part

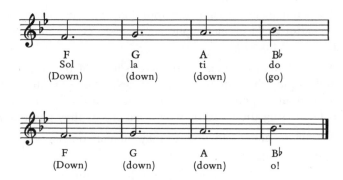

F	G	A	B♭
Sol	la	ti	do
(Down)	(down)	(down)	(go)

F	G	A	B♭
(Down)	(down)	(down)	o!

PROBLEM

Some students having special needs in learning to generalize and conceptualize in the regular music class.

KEY IDEAS

Provide many opportunities for students to make different kinds of applications to principles learned.

Provide for manipulations of symbols (abstractions) of sound.

Identify ways in which students can make their own application of a principle to other situations.

AN EXAMPLE

Objective: Having identified ABA form in a song and in objects within the environment, the student will create a composition in ABA form.

The teacher will

- Select a song with a form that is easily discernible, such as "Willowbee," page 92.

- Teach the students to sing the song, having them engage in the activities suggested by the words (walk) and stand in place during the other section, slapping their knees (*patschen*).

- Ask students how many different motions were made.

- Ask which motions were performed twice (knee slapping).

- Use squares to symbolize the first section (knee slapping) and a circle to symbolize the second section (walking).

- Ask students to place the symbols in the order that they made their motions (ABA or □ ○ □).

- Ask students to look around and find other patterns that are ABA. (A wall may have chalkboard, door, chalkboard, or a dress or shirt may have a design with this pattern. Or place a girl, boy, girl in ABA pattern.)

- Divide the class into groups of about five, giving each group different materials with which to create an original ABA composition. *Example:* (1) two rhythm patterns, such as

$$\frac{2}{4} \; \quad | \quad | \text{ and } \frac{2}{4} \quad | \quad |$$

(2) two types of rhythm instruments, such as metal and wood; (3) three tones from the xylophone, resonator bells, or piano.

- Tape-record the compositions, asking the class to evaluate them in terms of whether or not they are in ABA form.*

NOTE

In this example special needs in learning to generalize and conceptualize were provided for by

Leading students through a series of activities to help them generalize (listening, singing, moving, observing, and manipulating a visual symbol, applying the generalization to designs in the environment).
Providing opportunities to manipulate symbols.
Making a practical application of the generalization.

* Detailed suggestions for grouping may be found in Beer and Hoffman, *Teaching Music What, How, Why* (Morristown, N.J.: General Learning Press, 1973), pp. 83–101. Many ideas for creating compositions may be found on pp. 115–24 of the same work.

Willowbee

Southern Singing Game

This way   you   wil - low - bee,   Oh,   wil - low- bee,

Oh,   wil - low - bee,_____ __ This way   you   wil - low- bee,_____

All night_____ long.   *Fine*   Oh,_____   Walk - ing down   the

al - ley,   al - ley,   al - ley,   Walk - ing down   the

al - ley,   all   night   long.   Oh,___ *D.C. al Fine*

II

AN INSTRUCTIONAL PLAN

INTRODUCTION

The following instructional plan presents a broad framework to be adapted to suit individual situations and needs. Goals, short-term objectives, and examples of activities and procedures for achieving the objectives are presented.

GOALS

Goals are set forth in a Musical Response Sequence Chart, or nondependent hierarchy (see page 97). The basic goal, *to respond to music to the greatest possible extent,* is reached through singing, playing, moving, and listening. This text describes in detail how the *Musical Response Sequence Chart* can be used in planning annual goals and short term objectives for Singing (A), Playing (C), and Moving (D). These detailed suggestions are given for students performing at a very low level, and progress to a level where students can succeed in the regular music class. Although Music Reading (B) and Listening (E and F) are of equal importance and appear in the Sequence Chart, they are not explored in this text. Creativity is considered a thread that runs through all activities. The chart should be read from the bottom of the page to the top; goals labeled 1 (A-1, B-1, C-1, etc.) indicate beginning steps.

The color shading, from dark to light (easy to difficult), shows approximately the level of skill needed to take part in regular classroom music activities (Singing Goal A-4, Playing Goal C-4, Moving Goal D-5, Listening Goals E-1 and F-3).

For many students each goal will become an annual goal. These goals will lead the student from a level of awareness of musical sound to a level of critical judgment of his or her own musical performance and the musical performance of others.

Music goals should be a part of each exceptional child's individualized education program, not only because each exceptional child should have a program that includes music and the arts, but also because it is generally conceded that each goal contributes significantly to the child's general development and to development in the basic skills areas of

Academic achievement

Social adaptation

Psychomotor skills

Affective responsiveness

(See pages 17–40 on individualized education programs.)

In determining annual goals it is first essential to assess the student's singing, playing, moving, and listening behavior and then set forth a realistic annual goal in terms of the student's presenting behavior and his or her rate and style of learning.

INSTRUCTIONAL OBJECTIVES

Short-term instructional objectives are the means by which the annual goal is met. The instructional objectives reduce the annual goal to smaller, more manageable steps. These objectives must set forth observable and measurable evaluation criteria. When the student meets the evaluation criteria in a predetermined manner (two of three consecutive sessions, a percentage of accurate responses, etc.), mastery of the objective is confirmed, and the student is ready to go on to the next objective and to achieve eventual mastery of the annual goal.

Part II presents many examples of short-term instructional objectives under the Goals of Singing (A), Playing (C) and Moving (D). These examples include the following:

1. A statement of a short-term instructional objective
2. Suggested activities and procedures for achieving the objective

Musical Response Sequence Chart

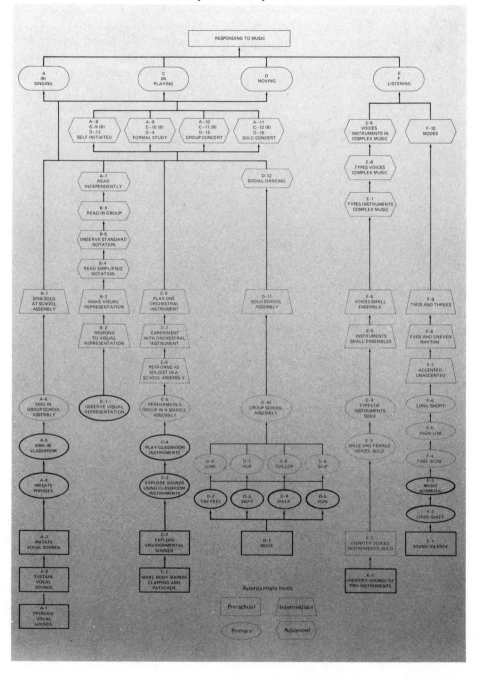

3. Equipment needed
4. Evaluation criteria

Although the authors hope that these examples will prove helpful to the reader, they are not intended to be all-encompassing or prescriptive. The individual needs of each child must dictate that child's program.

4 Singing

GOALS IN SINGING

Responding to music to the greatest possible extent by *singing* is a basic goal for all students, including the exceptional individual. Suggested annual goals which might derive from nondiscriminatory assessment of exceptional students are as follows:

A-1. Will produce vocal sounds when asked.

A-2. Will sustain vocal sounds when asked.

A-3. Will imitate simple vocal sounds when asked.

A-4. Will imitate short phrases when asked.

A-5. Will engage in regular classroom activities by singing when asked.

A-6. Will sing in a group in a school assembly or at a community function upon recommendation of the teacher.

A-7. Will sing a solo at a school or community function upon recommendation of the teacher.

A-8. Will engage in self-initiated vocal activities.

A-9. Will engage in formal vocal study.

A-10. Will sing as a member of a group in a formal concert setting.

A-11. Will sing a solo in a formal concert setting.

Goals in Singing

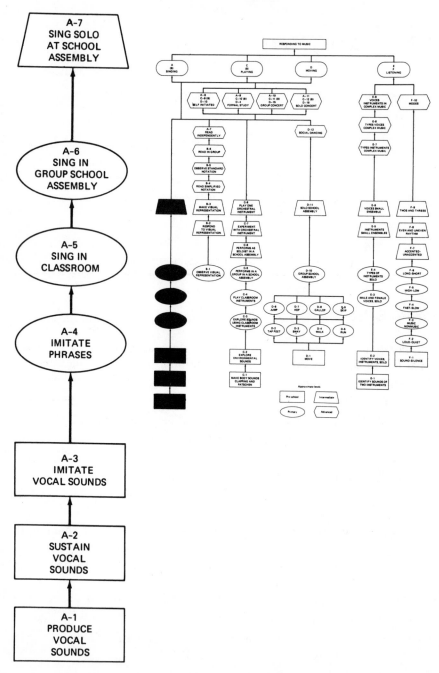

A-1 ANNUAL GOAL

The exceptional student will produce vocal sounds when asked.

MASTERING THE ANNUAL GOAL

Mastery of this annual goal may be achieved through a variety of short-term objectives. Key ideas contributing to success include

Using the appeal of music to stimulate response.

Encouraging response by rewarding any attempts made at vocalization.

Maintaining eye contact to aid concentration.

SHORT-TERM OBJECTIVE A-1-a

Objective: The student will produce a vocal sound in response to a vocal sound produced by the teacher.

The teacher will

- Take a position directly in front of one student and say or sing a repeated sound such as, "Ma—" or "Da—," urging the student to respond and trying to maintain eye contact with the student.

- Reward the student for each attempt.

Equipment needed: No special equipment is needed. It will be helpful to seat the students in a manner that will permit the teacher to take a position on eye level with the student.

Evaluation criteria: The student will produce any vocal sound in two of three consecutive sessions. The sounds may not necessarily be in imitation of the teacher.

SHORT-TERM OBJECTIVE A-1-b

Objective: The student will produce a vocal sound in response to the sound of music.

The teacher will

- Take a position directly in front of the student and sing. (The singing could be accompanied by guitar or Autoharp, or it could be unaccompanied. Try various types of songs, some legato and quiet, such as the familiar "Kum Ba Ya" or "Jacob's Ladder," page 102; or songs with a strong rhythmic appeal, such as the

familiar "Amen" or "Zum Gali Gali," page 102. In the latter type
try adding a finger-snapping accompaniment or a percussion instrument.)

Equipment needed: No special equipment is necessary unless an accompaniment is desired.

Evaluation criteria: The student will respond with some type of vocal
sound in two of three consecutive sessions. The sound may not necessarily
be in imitation of the teacher.

Jacob's Ladder

Spiritual

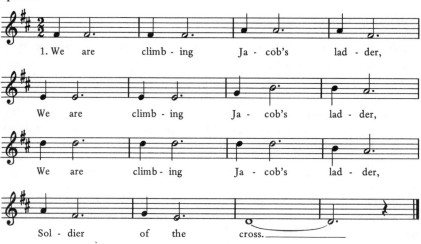

1. We are climb-ing Ja-cob's lad-der,

We are climb-ing Ja-cob's lad-der,

We are climb-ing Ja-cob's lad-der,

Sol-dier of the cross.

Zum Gali Gali

Israeli Folk Song

Zum ga-li, ga-li, ga-li, Zum ga-li, ga-li,

Zum ga-li, ga-li, ga-li, Zum ga-li, ga-li,

He-cha lutz le 'man a-vo-dah;_____ A-vo-dah le

'man he-cha-lutz,   Zum ga-li, ga-li, ga-li,   Zum ga-li, ga-li,

Zum ga-li, ga-li, ga-li,   Zum ga-li, ga-li,   Zum._____

The exceptional student will produce a vocal sound in response to the sound of music.

A-2 ANNUAL GOAL

The exceptional student will sustain vocal sounds when asked.

MASTERING THE ANNUAL GOAL

Mastery of this annual goal may be achieved through a variety of short-term objectives. Key ideas contributing to success include

Using the appeal of music to stimulate desired response.

Encouraging appropriate response by rewarding it immediately.

Stopping the student immediately when he or she makes an inappropriate response.

SHORT-TERM OBJECTIVE A-2-a

Objective: The student will sustain vocal sounds when given an aural and visual cue simultaneously.

The teacher will

- Sing or say a sustained sound such as "Ma—" or "Da—," accompanying the sound with a sustained motion—for example, pulling the arms apart or drawing a line on the chalkboard.
- Always make the sound and the motion simultaneous.
- Urge the student to sustain his or her sound.

Equipment needed: No special equipment is needed.

Evaluation criteria: The student will produce and sustain a vocal sound in response to a simultaneously given aural and visual cue. The sustained sound will not necessarily be in imitation of the teacher's.

SHORT-TERM OBJECTIVE A-2-b

Objective: The student will identify sounds in the environment that are sustained.

The teacher will

- Explain that some sounds heard every day are sustained sounds.
- Demonstrate a sustained sound using an example that is commonly found in the home, such as an alarm clock.
- Ask the students to indicate the duration of the alarm by standing when it starts and sitting when it stops. (Model as necessary.)
- Ask students to recall sounds that are sustained (fire whistle, cat meowing, etc.).
- Ask students to name sounds that are not sustained (dripping faucet, footsteps, etc.).

Equipment needed: A sound source available in most homes that is capable of producing a sustained sound.

Evaluation criteria: The student will name at least one sustained sound that is heard at home, in school, or in the community.

SHORT-TERM OBJECTIVE A-2-c

Objective: The student will produce a vocal sound, starting and stopping on aural cue.

The teacher will

- Produce a sustained sound on the melodica or organ or a tremolo on the xylophone.
- Ask the student to make his or her own vocal sound along with the instrument.
- Start with sounds of rather short duration and make them progressively longer.

Equipment needed: A sound source that is capable of producing a sound of various durations, such as a melodica, organ, harmonica, or xylophone.

Evaluation criteria: The student will sustain a vocal sound along with a sustained sound made by an instrument, starting and stopping approximately with the sound in two of three consecutive sessions. The sustained sound will not necessarily be in imitation of the original sound source.

A-3 ANNUAL GOAL

The exceptional student will imitate simple vocal sounds when asked.

MASTERING THE ANNUAL GOAL

Mastery of this annual goal may be achieved through a variety of short-term objectives. Key ideas contributing to success include

Using the appeal of music to stimulate response.
Modeling the required response accurately each time it is given.
Repeating the required response many times.
Making the practice periods short but frequent.

SHORT-TERM OBJECTIVE A-3-a

Objective: The exceptional student will imitate simple vocal sounds such as "Ma—" or "Da—," either speaking or singing them.
The teacher will

- Ask the student to listen carefully and repeat "Ma—."

Equipment needed: No special equipment is needed. The room should be arranged in such a way that the teacher can be directly in front of the student and on eye level so that the student can observe the teacher's lips and mouth.
Evaluation criteria: The student will reproduce the sound made by the teacher in two of three consecutive sessions. The sound may be either spoken or sung.

SHORT-TERM OBJECTIVE A-3-b

Objective: The student will imitate a simple vocal sound that is sung.
The teacher will

- Sing a simple sound such as "Ma—" or "Da—."
- Ask the student to make the same sound.
- Try singing the simple vocal sounds on different pitches to see whether the student is able to match one pitch more readily than another. (In the event that the student responds at a different pitch than given, try matching the student's pitch.)
- Try singing the student's name or such words as, "Come," "Stand," etc.

Equipment needed: No special equipment is needed.

Evaluation criteria: The student will imitate a simple vocal sound that is sung in two of three consecutive sessions.

SHORT-TERM OBJECTIVE A-3-c

Objective: The student will imitate a simple vocal sound as it recurs in a song.

The teacher will

- Sing such a song as "Old MacDonald Had a Farm," page 106 or "Pop Goes the Weasel," page 107, emphasizing the sound to be imitated ("chick, chick" or "pop") each time it occurs.

- Sing the sound that is to be imitated on the pitch on which it occurs in the song, asking the students to sing the word(s).

- Sing the song, asking the students to imitate the sound practiced as it occurs in the song.

Equipment needed: No special equipment is needed.

Evaluation criteria: The student will imitate a simple sound as it occurs in a song in two of three consecutive sessions.

Old MacDonald Had a Farm

Traditional American Folk Song

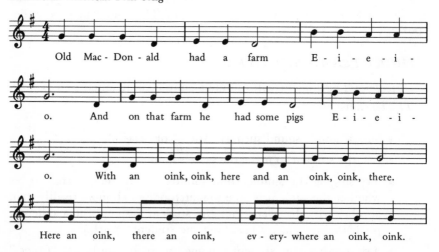

Old Mac-Don- ald   had a farm   E - i - e - i - o.

2. Chick, chick here, etc.
3. Quack, quack here, etc.
5. Baa, baa here, etc.
6. Moo, moo here, etc.

Pop, Goes the Weasel

Traditional American Folk Song

A   pen - ny   for   a   spool___ of thread, A

pen - ny   for   a   nee - dle   That's the way the

mon - ey goes,   Pop,   goes   the   wea - sel!

I've   no time   to   wait or sigh, And I've no time to   whee - dle,

On - ly time   to   say   good-by,   Pop,   goes   the   wea - sel!

A-4 ANNUAL GOAL

The exceptional student will imitate short phrases when asked.

MASTERING THE ANNUAL GOAL

Mastery of this annual goal may be achieved through a variety of short-term objectives. Key ideas contributing to success include

Using the appeal of music to stimulate desired response.

Modeling the required response accurately each time it is given.

Repeating the required response many times.

Making the practice periods short but frequent.

Adding interest by adding foot tapping or finger snapping as an unobtrusive accompaniment.

SHORT-TERM OBJECTIVE A-4-a

Objective: The student will imitate short random phrases.
The teacher will

- Sing a simple statement of fact, such as:

- Ask the student to echo the phrase.
- Try singing simple questions, asking the student to answer the question, such as:

Equipment needed: No special equipment is needed.

Evaluation criteria: The student will imitate short phrases, singing the rhythm and melody accurately in two of three consecutive sessions.

SHORT-TERM OBJECTIVE A-4-b

Objective: The student will imitate short phrases by singing the echo phrases in songs.
The teacher will

- Sing a song with an easy echo part, such as "Who Has A Green Dress?," page 109, asking students to listen carefully to determine which student is wearing the colors mentioned in the song.

- Ask students wearing the colors mentioned to stand as they hear their color in the song.
- Sing the song again.
- Ask the class to sing the response to the question asked in the song ("Who has a green dress? —has a green dress," etc.)
- Ask the individual wearing the color mentioned in the song to respond.

Equipment needed: No special equipment is needed.

Evaluation criteria: The student will accurately imitate the phrase sung by the teacher in two of three consecutive sessions.

Who Has A Green Dress?

Old Song Adapted

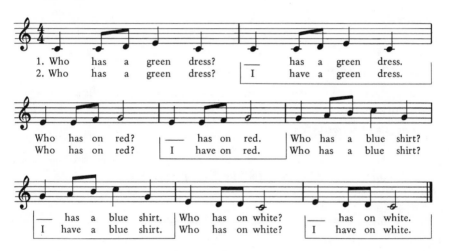

"Who Has A Green Dress?" adapted from "Who Has the Penny?," Angela Diller and Kate Stearns Page. From *A Pre-School Music Book,* copyright 1936, 1963.

Teach the echo phrases: "_____has a green dress."
"_____has on red."
"_____has a blue shirt."
"_____has on white."

My Little Ducklings

Words adapted
Austrian Folk Tune

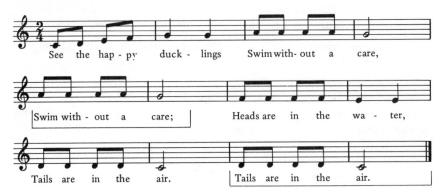

Teach the echo phrases: "Swim without a care"
"Tails are in the air"

SHORT-TERM OBJECTIVE A-4-c

Objective: The student will sing short repeated phrases in songs at the appropriate time.

The teacher will

- Select a song with one short phrase that is repeated several times, such as "Old Woman and the Pig," page 111.

- Ask the students to listen to determine what the song is about.

- Show a picture of a pig, horse, and cow.

- Ask the students to identify the animal mentioned in the song.

- Teach students to sing the phrase "Oink, oink, oink."

- Teach students a signal for starting and stopping the phrase "Oink, oink, oink."

- Sing the entire song, giving the signal for the class to sing the phrase "Oink, oink, oink."

Equipment needed: No special equipment is needed. It may help if Autoharp, guitar, or piano chords are played only on the phrase "Oink . . . ," thus helping to separate it from the rest of the song.

Evaluation criteria: The student will sing a short repeated phrase in a song. The phrase will be sung accurately and will be sung at the appropriate time in two of three consecutive sessions.

The Little Pig

Vermont Folk Song

Teach repeated phrases: "Oink, oink, oink."

A-5 ANNUAL GOAL

The exceptional student will engage in regular classroom music activities by singing when asked.

MASTERING THE ANNUAL GOAL

Mastery of this annual goal may be achieved through a variety of short-term objectives. Key ideas contributing to success include

Selecting songs that are appealing, usually without too many words.
Focusing attention on only one aspect of a song at one time.

Insisting upon students' listening to the song several times before trying to sing it (don't permit faking words).

Presenting an accurate model each time the model is repeated.

SHORT-TERM OBJECTIVE A-5-a

Objective: The student will engage in regular classroom music activities by singing only repeated phrases in a song.

The teacher will

- Select a song with a repeated phrase that is easy to identify and easy to sing, such as in the song "I Want to be Ready," page 113 (the phrase "Walk in Jerusalem just like John" is repeated four times).

- Ask students to observe the lines being drawn on the chalkboard as the song is sung.

- Sing the song, drawing the contour of the repeated phrase each time it occurs:

walk in Je-ru-sa-lem, etc.

- Ask if the lines were the same each time they were drawn (or part was sung).

- Teach the repeated phrase.

- Teach a signal for singing the repeated phrase and a signal for silence.

- Sing the entire song, asking the class to sing only on the repeated phrases.

- Invite students to sing along with the teacher on the entire song as soon as they have mastered the words and melody. (This is not a requirement for the exceptional student in mastery of this objective.)

Equipment needed: No special equipment is needed. However, playing the repeated phrase on bells or the piano is another way to emphasize it. In such an event an instrument would be needed, of course.

Evaluation criteria: The student will sing the repeated phrase accurately and at the appropriate time in two of three consecutive sessions.

I Want to Be Ready

Exceptional students will sing the repeated phrase:

"Walk in Jerusalem, just like John."

Mary Had a Baby

Spiritual

1. Ma-ry had a Ba - by   Yes,   Lord,   Ma-ry had a Ba - by

Yes,   my   Lord,   Ma - ry   had   a   Ba - by   Yes   Lord'

The   peo - ple   keep   a - com - in'   and the   train   done   gone.

2. *Laid Him in a manger,* Yes, Lord
   Laid Him in a manger, Yes, my Lord,
   Laid Him in a manger, Yes, Lord!
   The people keep a comin' and the train done gone.
3. *Shepherds came to see Him,* Yes, Lord,
   Shepherds came to see Him, Yes, my Lord,
   Shepherds came to see Him, Yes, my Lord!
   The people keep a comin' and the train done gone.

Exceptional students will sing the repeated phrases:

1. "Mary had a Baby"
2. "Laid Him in a manger"
3. "Shepherds came to see Him"

The Gang's All Here

Words by W. S. Gilbert
(adapted)
Music by Arthur S. Sullivan

Hail!   Hail!_____   the   gang's   all   here,

Nev - er   mind   the   weath - er,   Here   we   are   to - geth - er.

Teach the repeated phrase:

"Hail! Hail! the gang's all here."

SHORT-TERM OBJECTIVE A-5-b

Objective: The student will engage in regular classroom music activities by singing only the refrain of a song.

The teacher will

- Select a song having several stanzas and a refrain, such as "One More River," page 116.
- Establish a specific purpose for listening. For example, in "One More River" ask students to identify a phrase that is repeated many times ("One more river").
- Establish a second purpose for listening, such as asking students to recall the animals that are mentioned.
- Establish a third purpose for listening, such as asking students to recall the number of animals of each kind.
- Teach the refrain.
- Teach the signal for starting and stopping.
- Sing the entire song, asking the class to sing only the refrain upon signal.
- Invite students to sing along with the teacher on the entire song as soon as they have mastered the words. (This is not a requirement for the exceptional student in mastery of this objective.)

Equipment needed: No special equipment is needed unless an accompaniment is desired.

Evaluation criteria: The student will sing the refrain of a song accurately and at the appropriate time in two of three consecutive sessions.

One More River

Spiritual

2. The animals came two by two, One more river to cross.
   The elephant and kangaroo, One more river to cross.
3. The animals came three by three, One more river to cross.
   The baboon and the chimpanzee, One more river to cross.
4. The animals came four by four, One more river to cross.
   The hippopotamus got stuck in the door, One more river to cross.
5. The animals came five by five, One more river to cross.
   The bees came swarming from the hive, One more river to cross.

The exceptional student will sing the refrain:

"One more river, And that wide river is Jordan,
One more river, There's one more river to cross."

Goodbye Ol' Paint

Traditional Cowboy Song

REFRAIN

Good - bye, ol' Paint, I'm a - leav - in' Chey - enne,

Good - bye, ol' Paint, I'm a - leav - in' Chey - enne.

My foot in the stir - rup, my po - ny won't, stan',____

I'm a - leav - in' Chey - enne an' I'm off for Mon - tan'.____

D.C. al Fine

2. I'm a ridin' ol' Paint an' a-leadin' ol' Dan,
   Goodbye, little Annie, I'm off for Montan'
3. My foot in the stir-rup, my bridle in han',
   I'm a-leavin' Cheyenne an' I'm off for Montan.

The exceptional student will sing the Refrain;
  "Good bye, ol' Paint, I'm a-leavin' Cheyenne,
  Goodbye, ol' Paint, I'm a-leavin' Cheyenne."

The exceptional student will sing the refrain:

"Good bye, ol' Paint, I'm a-leavin' Cheyenne,
Goodbye, ol' Paint, I'm a-leavin' Cheyenne."

SHORT-TERM OBJECTIVE A-5-c

Objective: The exceptional student will engage in regular classroom
music activities by singing entire songs.
The teacher will

- Select an appealing song that has few words and a limited range, such as "I'm Gonna Sing," page 118.

- Identify one very obvious characteristic of the words or the music and focus students' attention on it by asking a question such as "What is the main idea of this song?" or "What is the title of this song?"

- Identify a specific purpose for listening for a total of about three times.

- Use visual aids to help students remember the words and the order of persons, actions, or places.

- Ask the class to sing only part of the song at first (repeated phrases, refrain, etc.)

- Ask the class to sing the entire song.

Equipment needed: No special equipment is needed. Visual aids should be available as needed, however.

Evaluation criteria: The student will sing the entire song accurately along with other students in a regular classroom.

I'm Gonna Sing

Spiritual

1. I'm gon-na sing when the spir-it says, "sing,"
   I'm gon-na sing when the spir-it says, "sing,"____
   I'm gon-na sing when the spir-it says, "sing,"
   And o-bey the spir-it of the Lord.

2. I'm gonna shout...
3. I'm gonna preach...
4. I'm gonna pray...

Exceptional students will sing the entire song with the regular class.

The Old Ark's A-moverin'

Spiritual

Oh, the old ark's a - mov-er- in', a mov-er-in' a mov-er-in',

The old ark's a - mov- er- in, And I'm go- ing home *Fine*

See that sis - ter dressed so fine?

She has - 'nt got re - li - gion in - a her mind.
D.C. al Fine

2. See that brother dressed in gray?
   The Devil's gonna come and take him away.
3. See that sister walking slow?
   Old Satan's gonna grab her by the big toe.
4. Tain't but one thing grieves my mind,
   Those sinners went away and left me behind.
5. Old ark, she reeled, old ark rocked.
   The old ark landed on the mountain top.

The exceptional students will sing the refrain at first, but with the use of pictures or visual aids could soon sing the entire song with the regular classroom.

This Train

Spiritual

1. This train is bound for glo- ry, this train,_____

This train is bound for glo- ry, this train._____

This train is bound for glo-ry, If you ride it, you must be ho-ly, This train is bound for glo-ry, this train.

2. This train won't pull no extras, this train
   This train won't pull no extras,
   Don't pull nothin' but the midnight special,
3. This train don't pull no sleepers, this train,
   This train don't pull no sleepers,
   Don't pull nothin' but the righteous people,
4. This train don't pull no jokers, this train,
   This train don't pull no jokers,
   Don't pull nothin' but the righteous people,

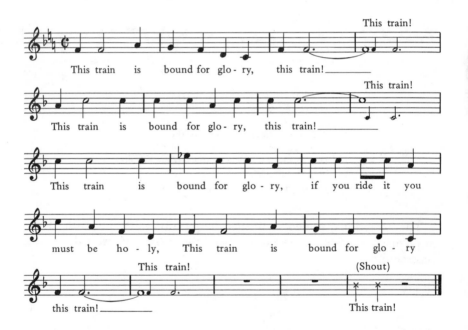

This train is bound for glo-ry, this train! This train!

This train is bound for glo-ry, this train! This train!

This train is bound for glo-ry, if you ride it you must be ho-ly, This train is bound for glo-ry

This train! this train! (Shout) This train!

1. The exceptional student will first sing the first and last phrases:
   "This trains is bound for glory, this train"
2. The exceptional student will sing the first and last stanzas.
3. The exceptional student will sing the entire song with the regular classroom.

5 *Playing*

GOALS IN PLAYING

Responding to music to the greatest possible extent by *playing* is a basic goal for all students, including the exceptional individual. Suggested annual goals which might derive from nondiscriminatory assessment of exceptional students:

    C-1. Will produce such body sounds as foot tapping, hand clapping, knee slapping (*patschen*), etc. when asked.

    C-2. Will explore environmental sounds, identifying like and unlike sounds.

    C-3. Will explore sounds using classroom instruments, identifying like and unlike sounds.

    C-4. Will engage in regular classroom music activities by playing classroom instruments when asked. NOTE: Sample short-term objectives, C-4-a through C-4-k, are concerned with rhythm instruments. Sample short-term objectives, C-4-l through C-4-n, deal with playing melody instruments.

    C-5. Will perform in a group in a school assembly or community function upon recommendation of the teacher.

Goals in Playing

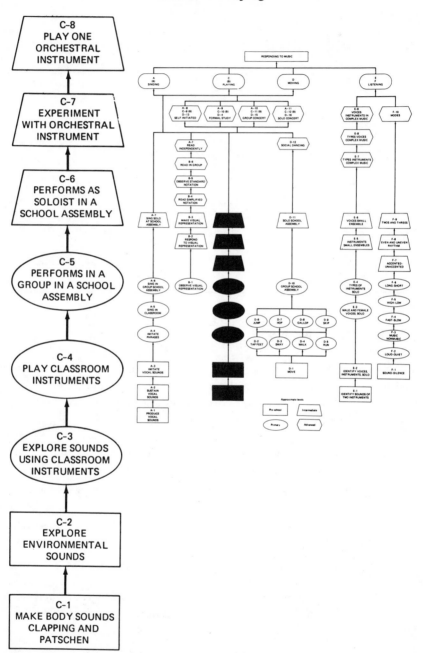

C-6. Will perform as soloist in a school assembly or community function upon recommendation of the teacher.

C-7. Will experiment with orchestral instruments. The instruments should be from at least two of the four families of orchestral instruments.

C-8. Will play one orchestral instrument or the piano in the regular classes of instrumental music instruction.

C-9. Will engage in self-initiated instrumental music activities.

C-10. Will engage in formal instrumental study.

C-11. Will perform in an instrumental group in a formal concert setting.

C-12. Will perform as instrumental soloist in a formal concert setting.

C-1 ANNUAL GOAL

The exceptional student will produce such body sounds as foot tapping, hand clapping, knee slapping, etc. when asked.

MASTERING THE ANNUAL GOAL

Mastery of this annual goal may be achieved through a variety of short-term objectives. Key ideas contributing to success include

Using the appeal of rhythm. Chanting, singing, or playing an instrument will often motivate the most reluctant student to respond.

Modeling the required response when necessary, but striving to make the student independent of the model.

Assisting students physically when necessary, but striving to make the student responsive to directions.

Encouraging preverbal students to attempt to say the chant in cooperation with the speech therapist.

SHORT-TERM OBJECTIVE C-1-a

Objective: The student will produce a specific body sound when the direction is rhythmically chanted.

The teacher will

● Chant rhythmically,

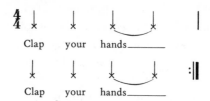

demonstrating the act of clapping and taking a position directly in front of the student.

- Physically assist any students who do not respond.
- Call for other responses by rhythmically chanting such words as "Tap your foot," "Slap your knees," etc.

Equipment needed: No special equipment is needed. The students should be seated in such a way that the teacher can take a position directly in front of each student.

Evaluation criteria: The student will respond to the chanted direction in two of three consecutive sessions.

SHORT-TERM OBJECTIVE C-1-b

Objective: The student will produce a specific body sound when the direction is sung.

The teacher will

- Sing a song whose words demand a response of producing a body sound, such as "Rhythm Game" or "If You're Happy," page 125.
- Demonstrate the act of clapping and take a position directly in front of each student.
- Physically assist those who do not respond readily.
- Call for other responses by singing other words, such as "Tap your feet," etc.

Equipment needed: No special equipment is needed. The students should be seated in such a way that the teacher can take a position directly in front of the students.

Evaluation criteria: The student will respond by producing a specific body sound when the direction is sung in two of three consecutive sessions.

If You're Happy

Traditional

If   you're hap-py and you know it, clap your   hands, (clap,   clap)

If you're   hap-py and you know it, clap your   hands, (clap,   clap)

If   you're hap-py and you know it,   then your   face will sure-ly show it,

If   you're hap-py and you know it, clap your   hands. (clap,   clap.)

The exceptional student will produce a specific body sound when the direction is sung.

Rhythm Game

Words adapted
Italian folk tune

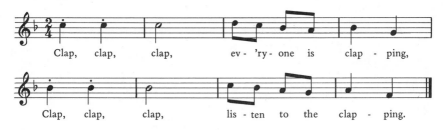

Clap,   clap,   clap,   ev - 'ry- one is   clap - ping,

Clap,   clap,   clap,   lis - ten to   the   clap - ping.

Call for other responses, such as "Tap your feet."

The exceptional student will produce a specific body sound when the direction is sung.

SHORT-TERM OBJECTIVE C-1-c

Objective: The student will produce a specific body sound, responding as directed to a specific instrumental sound.

The teacher will

- Play a tone block in a repetitious rhythm, chanting and modeling the directions.

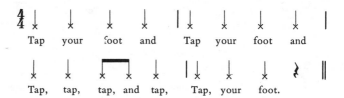

- Continue to play the tone block but stop chanting and modeling, giving one verbal direction to tap the foot.
- Make a tape recording of an instrument of a contrasting sound (finger cymbal or tambourine) in a repetitious rhythm.
- Chant and model the directions.

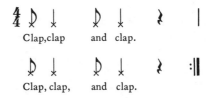

- Play the tambourine without chanting and modeling, giving a verbal direction to clap.
- Follow the same procedure for slapping the kness to repetitious rhythm played on the drum.

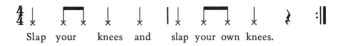

- Make a tape recording of each of the three instruments, asking students to respond in the manner practiced:

  tone block—tap foot
  tambourine—clap hands
  drum—slap knees

Equipment needed: Three rhythm instruments of different tone qualities, such as tone block, tambourine, and drum. In order to model the activities it will be necessary to prepare a tape recording of the instrumental sounds.

Evaluation criteria: The student will respond as practiced to the sound of each instrument in two of three consecutive sessions. The response need not be in strict rhythm.

C-2 ANNUAL GOAL

The exceptional student will explore environmental sounds, identifying like and unlike sounds.

MASTERING THE ANNUAL GOAL

Mastery of this annual goal may be achieved through a variety of short-term objectives. Key ideas contributing to success include

Remembering that the intent of the activities is to develop sensitivity to sounds.

Treating each sound that the student produces seriously, listening intently so that the activity elicits only positive responses.

Maintaining a quiet atmosphere so that each student's sound can be heard distinctly.

SHORT-TERM OBJECTIVE C-2-a

Objective: The student will explore environmental sounds, producing two unlike sounds by tapping different parts of a chair.

The teacher will

- Be seated on a chair in front of the class and ask the students to listen carefully to the sound.
- Tap the back of the chair and then the leg.
- Ask the students whether the sounds are alike or different.
- Ask one student to tap a part of the chair on which he or she is seated.
- Ask the student to tap another part of the chair.
- Ask the class to determine whether the sounds are alike or different.
- Ask other students to find two different sounds by tapping their chairs.

Equipment needed: No special equipment is needed. The students should be seated in such a way as to see the teacher.

Evaluation criteria: The student will differentiate between like and unlike sounds when given two sounds. The response will be accurate in two of three consecutive sessions.

SHORT-TERM OBJECTIVE C-2-b

Objective: The student will explore environmental sounds using an assigned object to produce two unlike sounds.

The teacher will

- Assign each student to one object in the room—a table, a wastebasket, a door, etc.
- Ask each student to find at least two different sounds that can be produced by striking the object.
- Ask students to find other ways of producing sound, such as rubbing, scraping, etc.
- Ask each student to produce two sounds on the assigned object.
- Ask the class to determine whether the sounds are alike or different.

Equipment needed: No special equipment is needed.

Evaluation criteria: The student will differentiate between like and unlike sounds when given two examples. This will be achieved in two of three consecutive sessions.

SHORT-TERM OBJECTIVE C-2-c

Objective: The student will explore environmental sounds within a confined area, producing two unlike sounds.

The teacher will

- Assign each student to a defined area in the classroom.
- Ask each student to produce as many different sounds as possible within the assigned area.
- Ask each student to produce just two sounds, using only objects from within the assigned area.
- Ask the class to determine whether the sounds are alike or different.

Equipment needed: No special equipment is needed.

Evaluation criteria: The student will differentiate between like and unlike sounds when given two examples. This will be achieved in two of three consecutive sessions.

SHORT-TERM OBJECTIVE C-2-d

Objective: The student will explore environmental sounds using an object brought from home, producing like and unlike sounds.

The teacher will

- Ask each student to bring one object from home on which it is possible to produce at least two different sounds.
- Ask each student in turn to produce two different sounds on the object brought from home and ask the class to determine whether the sounds are different.

Equipment needed: Students will bring needed equipment. In the event that all students do not bring objects, the teacher may wish to have some household objects available, such as an eggbeater, lids of cooking pans, etc.

Evaluation criteria: The student will differentiate between like and unlike sounds when given two examples. This will be achieved in two of three consecutive sessions.

C-3 ANNUAL GOAL

The exceptional student will explore sounds using classroom instruments, identifying like and unlike sounds.

MASTERING THE ANNUAL GOAL

Mastery of this annual goal may be achieved through a variety of short-term objectives. Key ideas contributing to success include

Remembering that students are learning to manipulate instruments. Do not hurry.

Adapting instruments to care for physical handicaps.

Encouraging students to explore the full range of tone color and pitch.

Listening intently. Each exploratory effort is important.

SHORT-TERM OBJECTIVE C-3-a

Objective: The student will explore sounds using classroom instruments, producing two unlike sounds on a rhythm instrument.

The teacher will

- Demonstrate two different ways to produce a sound on a drum (tap the head and then the body of the drum).
- Ask each student to try to find a different way to produce a sound on the drum (scratching the head, striking with a mallet, etc.)
- Ask the students whether each consecutive sound is like the preceding one or different.
- Follow the same procedure using other rhythm instruments.

Equipment needed: A drum and other instruments such as a triangle, tone block, cymbal, or tambourine.

Evaluation criteria: The student will differentiate between like and unlike sounds when they are produced consecutively on one instrument. The student will accurately identify the sounds in two of three successive sessions.

SHORT-TERM OBJECTIVE C-3-b

Objective: The student will explore sound using classroom instruments, determining whether the sound is produced on a drum or a wooden or metal instrument.

The teacher will

- Assign one group of students metal instruments (triangles, cymbals, cow bells, etc.), another group wooden instruments (tone blocks, claves, etc.), and another group drums.
- Ask students to look carefully at the other instruments in their group to see whether there is anything alike about the instruments in their group. (It may be necessary to guide student's observation by asking leading questions.)
- Ask students with metal instruments to play them one at a time to determine whether there is anything about their sound that is alike. (The teacher may call the sound a "ringing sound.")
- Follow the same procedure with other groups.
- Ask students to close their eyes, explaining that when anyone is tapped on the shoulder, that person will play his or her instru-

ment. The class will determine to which group the instrument belongs.

OR

- Tape-record the individual instruments, asking students to classify the sounds by verbal response or by pointing to the appropriate instrument.

Equipment needed: Drums, instruments made of metal, and those made of wood. If instruments are not available, substitute large nails and metal pipes hung on a frame for the metal sound; an assortment of seven-inch lengths of dowel of various thicknesses, broomsticks, etc. for the wooden instrument sound; and coffee cans of various sizes (with plastic lids) for the drum sound.

Evaluation criteria: Upon hearing the sound, the student will determine whether a specific sound is produced on a drum, a rhythm instrument made of metal, or one made of wood. The identification will be made upon hearing the sound, even though the instrument cannot be seen. The student will correctly identify the group to which the instrument belongs in two of three consecutive sessions.

SHORT-TERM OBJECTIVE C-3-c

Objective: The student will explore sounds using classroom instruments by finding and playing the highest and lowest tones on a keyboard- or xylophone-type instrument.

The teacher will

- Play the lowest tones on the piano, melody bells, chord organ, or other available keyboard instrument. (Melodicas may be used for this activity provided they have the tube attachment so that they can be placed on the desk as they are played.)
- Ask the students to find the lowest tones on their instruments. (If only one piano or set of bells is available, ask one student to find the lowest tones on the instrument, having the class verify accuracy.)
- Follow the same procedure for finding the highest tones, reminding the students that the high tones are always on the right.

Equipment needed: At least one keyboard instrument or set of melody bells; more if possible so that many students can participate. If mallet instruments are used, have one mallet for each hand to emphasize laterality. Hand splints may assist a weak mallet grasp.

Evaluation criteria: The student will correctly find and play the highest and the lowest tones on a keyboard- or xylophone-type instrument in two of three consecutive sessions.

SHORT-TERM OBJECTIVE C-3-d

Objective: The student will explore sound using classroom instruments, locating and playing groups of three and two black keys on a keyboard- or xylophone-type instrument, playing them from high to low when asked.

The teacher will

- Arrange students in such a way that they can see the keyboard or melody bells, and point out and play one group of three black keys.
- Ask a student to find and play one group of three black keys.
- Ask a student to find and play another set of three black keys.
- Ask a student to find and play the highest set of three black keys.
- Ask a student to play the groups of three black keys from high to low (right to left).
- Follow the same procedure for locating and playing the groups of two black keys from high to low.

Equipment needed: At least one keyboard instrument and/or a set of melody bells; more if possible so that many students can participate. If melody bells are used, have one mallet for each hand so that laterality can be emphasized.

Evaluation criteria: The student will play groups of either two or three black keys on a keyboard- or xylophone-type instrument, moving from high to low. The student will perform the task accurately in two of three consecutive sessions.

SHORT-TERM OBJECTIVE C-3-e

Objective: The student will explore sound using classroom instruments, locating and playing groups of three and two black keys on a keyboard- or xylophone-type instrument, playing them from low to high when asked.

See Objective C-3-d for procedure, equipment, and criteria for evaluation.

SHORT-TERM OBJECTIVE C-3-f

Objective: The student will explore sound using classroom instruments, improvising on black keys of a keyboard instrument or a xylophone-type instrument and using tones that go from high to low and low to high pitches.

The teacher will

- Improvise freely on the black keys, moving from low to high and high to low, playing clusters (three or two tones simultaneously) single tones, etc.
- Ask the students to play using black keys only.
- Encourage students to experiment with different ways to play from high to low and low to high. Praise those who find different ways to play.
- Identify two students to improvise together, asking students to listen to the sound of the two instruments played together, asking such questions as "Is one louder than the other?," "Is one faster than the other?," and "Are keys played singly or simultaneously?"

Equipment needed: At least two keyboards or xylophone-type instruments. Electronic keyboards with headsets are ideal.

Evaluation criteria: The student will improvise on a keyboard- or xylophone-type instrument, employing tones that move from high to low and low to high pitches. Students will perform as asked in two of three consecutive sessions.

C-4 ANNUAL GOAL

The exceptional student will engage in regular classroom music activities by playing classroom instruments when asked.

MASTERING THE ANNUAL GOAL

Mastery of this annual goal may be achieved through a variety of short-term objectives. Key ideas contributing to success include

Being consistent in modeling the manner in which each instrument is to be played.

Giving physical assistance to students who need it.

Mastering the skill of playing one instrument before introducing another.

Using word rhythms to describe the method of playing or the sound produced.

Insisting that students learn to start and stop playing on an aural or visual cue.

Employing word rhythms. Speaking words of a song or names, phrases, etc. usually helps.

Playing only a few instruments at one time to avoid a cluttered sound.

Playing rhythm instruments more softly than the voices are singing, to serve as an accompaniment.

Pantomiming playing in rhythm.

Singing letter names when playing melody instruments.

Playing only repeated fragments on melody instruments.

Simplifying parts of melody instruments.

Assigning only one fragment, phrase, or section to melody instrument players.

SHORT-TERM OBJECTIVE C-4-a

Objective: The student will play a drum as an accompaniment to a song, when given a model.

The teacher will

- Take a position directly in front of one student and play a drum accompaniment to a song with rhythmic appeal, such as "Dry Bones," page 134. (A bongo drum, placed between the knees and played with the fingers, is an easy approach for many students.)
- Hand the student another bongo drum, and ask the student to "mirror" the manner in which the drum is played.

Equipment needed: Two bongo drums and a song to be sung, or one that is recorded.

Evaluation criteria: The student will imitate the manner in which the teacher is playing the bongo in two or three consecutive sessions.

Dry Bones

Traditional

E - ze -kiel cried, "Them   dry___ bones" E - ze - kiel cried, "Them

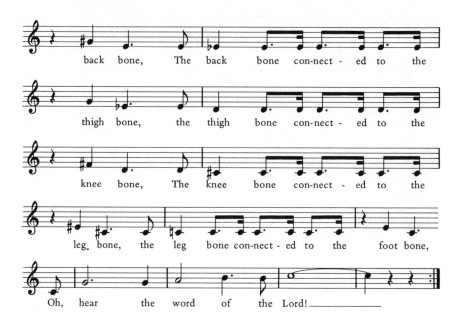

back bone, The back bone con-nect - ed to the

thigh bone, the thigh bone con-nect - ed to the

knee bone, The knee bone con-nect - ed to the

leg bone, the leg bone con-nect - ed to the foot bone,

Oh, hear the word of the Lord!

The exceptional student will play a drum as an accompaniment to a song when given a model.

SHORT-TERM OBJECTIVE C-4-b

Objective: The student will play a tone-block accompaniment to a song when given a model.

The teacher will

- Strike the tone block with the wooden mallet, asking students to observe.

- Hand the tone block to a student, asking the student to tap the tone block with the mallet.

- Ask another student to tap the tone block in a different manner.

- Ask other students to try to tap the tone block in different ways.

- Sing the refrain of a song such as "Riding in a Buggy," page 137, tapping the tone block on the large part of the instrument (in the traditional manner).

- Hand a student another tone block and ask that student to play in imitation.

- Sing the verse of the song and play the tone block first on the large part (in the traditional manner) and then on the handle. (This will give the effect of clip-clop.)
- Ask a student to play a tone block in the same manner.
- Sing the entire song, asking some students to play on the verse, playing on the handle and then on the large part, and asking others to play only on the refrain, playing in the traditional manner.

Equipment needed: Several tone blocks with mallets.

Evaluation criteria: The student will play a tone-block accompaniment to a song in at least one of two demonstrated ways. The student will perform the activity in two of three consecutive sessions.

Riding In a Buggy

Traditional Folk Song

The exceptional student will play a tone-block accompaniment when given a model.

SHORT-TERM OBJECTIVE C-4-c

Objective: The student will play the tambourine as an accompaniment to a song when given a model.

The teacher will

- Play a rhythm that combines tapping and shaking the tambourine as an introduction to a song, and use the same rhythm as an accompaniment throughout the song. A song such as "Tum Balalaika," page 138, could be introduced with the following pattern:

- Sing the song, playing the tambourine accompaniment; ask students to pantomime playing a tambourine in the same manner.
- Hand a tambourine to students who are able to play the rhythm, asking them to model for the class.

Equipment needed: Several tambourines and a suitable song or recording.

Evaluation criteria: The student will play a tambourine accompaniment to a song in the same manner as the teacher has played. The student will play correctly in two of three consecutive sessions.

Tum Balalaika

Yiddish Folk Song

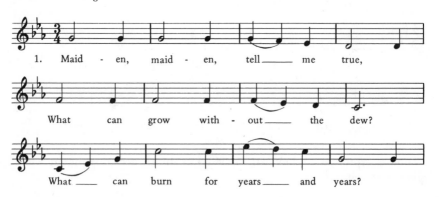

What ____ can cry and shed ____ no tears?

REFRAIN

Tum - ba - la, tum - ba - la, tum - ba - la - lai - ka,

tum - ba - la - tum - ba - la tum - ba - la - lai - ka,

tum - ba - la - lai - ka, Tum - ba - la - lai - ka,

Tum ba - la - lai - ka, Tum ba - la - lai - ka.

2. Silly lad, the answer true;
A stone can grow without the dew.
What can burn for years and years.
A heart can cry and shed no tears.

The exceptional student will play the tambourine as an accompaniment to a song when given a model.

SHORT-TERM OBJECTIVE C-4-d

Objective: The student will play a rhythm instrument that is named in a song, selecting it from among three instruments.

The teacher will

- Select a song whose words indicate a specific rhythm instrument accompaniment, such as "The Drum," page 140.
- Sing the song, asking the students to determine which instrument is mentioned in the song.
- Sing the song again, playing the drum, and ask students to pantomime playing the drum.
- Identify a student who is following the direction and ask that student to play the drum.

- Identify other students to play the drum as the class pantomimes.
- Use as many drums as possible (as long as the drum is played as an *accompaniment*, softer than the voice part).
- Substitute names of other instruments—for example, "Hear the tambourine" or "Rhythm sticks go click."
- Arrange three instruments on a table. Sing a song that names one of the instruments. Ask students to select and play the instrument named in the song.
- Repeat the procedure for other instruments.

Equipment needed: At least three different rhythm instruments, such as drums, tambourines, cymbals, tone blocks, or claves.

Evaluation criteria: The student will select the correct instrument, choosing from among three instruments. The student will play the instruments, although not necessarily in strict rhythm. The selection will be accurate in two of three consecutive sessions.

The Drum

Alice S. Beer

The exceptional student will play a rhythm instrument that is named in a song.

Big Bass Drum

Traditional

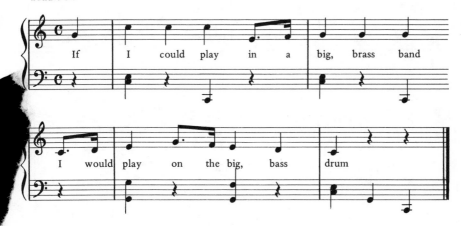

If I could play in a big, brass band
I would play on the big, bass drum

2. If I could play in the big, brass band
   I would play on the tambourine.

The exceptional student will play a rhythm instrument that is named in a song.

Cymbals

Words and music by Francis Anderson

Cym-bals make an aw-ful crash, but on-ly if you want to smash.

If you tap them light-ly, They will ans-wer back so soft-ly.

The Triangle

Words adapted
Italian Folk Tune

Ring, ring, ring, tri - ang - les are ring - ing,

Ring, ring, ring, lis - ten to them ring.

The exceptional student will play a rhythm instrument that is named in a song.

Tap On Your Drum, Amigo

Words and music by Carla Barnes

Tap on your drum, a - mi - go, tap on your drum.

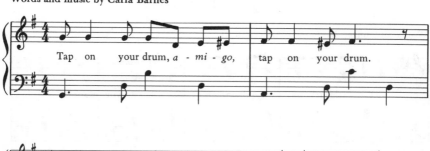

Tap on your drum, a - mi - go, tap on your drum.

You can tap with your fin-gers, you can tap with your toes,

Tap out a rhy-thm, ni - ño, show how it goes!

2. Tap on your sticks, *amigo,* tap on your sticks.
   Tap on your sticks, *amigo,* tap on your sticks.
   You can tap on your sticks and you can tap on your chair,
   Tap out a rhythm, *niño,* that's how we share!
         AMIGO means friend
         NIÑO means little one

The exceptional student will play a rhythm instrument that is named in a song.

SHORT-TERM OBJECTIVE C-4-e

Objective: The student will play a rhythm instrument as an accompaniment to a song, playing only for the duration of the song.

The teacher will

- Select a song with a marked rhythm.

- Sing the song, playing the drum as an accompaniment. Ask students to pantomime playing the drum as they listen. Caution them to start and stop with the teacher.

- Identify a successful student to play the drum accompaniment as the song is sung and as the class pantomimes, cautioning him or her to play only during the song.

- Repeat the procedure until each student has had an opportunity to play the drum as an accompaniment to the song. (More than one drummer may be used as long as the drums do not sound louder than the song. Be sure that the drum is played only for the duration of the song.)

- Follow the same procedure for other rhythm instruments, stressing the importance of starting and stopping with the song.

Equipment needed: At least one of each instrument introduced. It is best to introduce one type of instrument at a time, since several different instruments produce a cluttered sound.

Evaluation criteria: The student will play a rhythm instrument for the duration of a song, starting and stopping correctly in two of three consecutive sessions. The playing may not necessarily be in strict rhythm.

SHORT-TERM OBJECTIVE C-4-f

Objective: The student will play a specified rhythm-instrument accompaniment for a specified phrase or section of a song.

The teacher will

- Select a song with a marked rhythm and easily discernible phrases or sections, such as "Hop Up, My Ladies!," page 144 (the refrain changes in both rhythm and pitch level).
- Sing the song and play the tone block on the refrain only, asking students to clap when tone block is heard.
- Observe the students and select one who has responded as directed to play tone block on the refrain.
- Repeat the procedure until each student has had an opportunity to play the tone block on the refrain.

Equipment needed: Tone block or other rhythm instrument appropriate to the song.

Evaluation criteria: The student will play a specified rhythm instrument for a specified duration, starting and stopping correctly in two of three consecutive sessions. The playing may not necessarily be in strict rhythm.

Hop Up, My Ladies!

American Folk Song

1. Did you ev - er go to meet - ing, Un - cle Joe, Un - cle Joe?

Did you ev-er go to meet-ing Un-cle Joe"___ Did you

ev-er go to meet-ing Un-cle Joe, Un-cle Joe?

Don't mind the weath-er, so the wind don't blow.

REFRAIN

Hop up, my la - dies, three in a row,

Hop up, my la - dies, three in a row,

Hop up, my la - dies, three in a row,

Don't mind the weath-er, so the wind don't blow.

2. Will your horse carry double, Uncle Joe, Uncle Joe? (3 times)
   Don't mind the weather, so the wind don't blow.
3. Is your horse a single-footer, Uncle Joe, Uncle Joe" (3 times)
   Don't mind the weather so the wind don't blow.

SHORT-TERM OBJECTIVE C-4-g

Objective: The student will play a rhythm instrument in the rhythm of his or her name.

The teacher will

- Chant one student's name, simultaneously tapping the rhythm of the name on a drum or tone block. It may be helpful to start by tapping a steady beat with the foot, as,

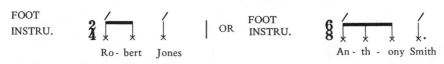

- Ask the student whose name is chanted to stand beside the drum and repeat his or her name with the teacher and the drum.
- Ask the student to chant his or her name as he or she plays the appropriate rhythm on the drum.
- Ask the student to play the rhythm of his or her name without saying the name aloud.
- Follow the same procedure for other students.
- Play the rhythm of a student's name without chanting, asking students whose name matches the drum to stand. Some students may have the same rhythm, as,

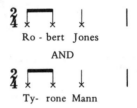

Ro - bert Jones

AND

Ty- rone Mann

- Reward students who recognize the rhythm of their name by permitting them to play the rhythm of a name for their classmates to recognize.

Equipment needed: Timpani or a bass drum with beaters is ideal; however, the activity can be successfully completed with a small drum or tone block or even rhythm sticks.

Evaluation criteria: The student will play the rhythm of his or her name on a rhythm instrument accurately in two of three consecutive sessions.

SHORT-TERM OBJECTIVE C-4-h

Objective: The student will play rhythm instruments in the rhythm of a chant (or old saying), adding improvised rhythm-instrument parts.

The teacher will

- Select an old saying or a short poem that has a singsong rhythm, as,

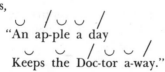

"An ap-ple a day
Keeps the Doc-tor a-way."

- Chant the words, simultaneously playing the rhythm on a drum or another rhythm instrument, as,

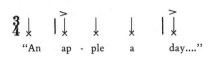

- Ask the students to chant with the rhythmic accompaniment.

- Repeat as many times as needed to master the words.

- Select a few students to play the rhythm-instrument accompaniment, all playing the same-sounding instruments, such as tone blocks *or* drums *or* others.

- Pick out one word or a short phrase and play it intermittently on an instrument of contrasting sound as the class chants the entire saying, as,

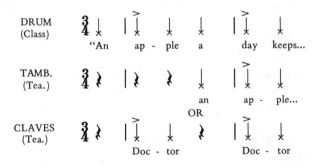

- Ask a student to pick out a word or phrase to play on an instrument of contrasting sound, playing it intermittently at his or her discretion (or in imitation of the teacher).

- Ask other students to add a part intermittently. (It may be necessary to play only one added part at a time so that the sound will not be lost.)

- Ask students to play their instrumental parts without chanting the words.

Equipment needed: A variety of instruments, preferably one for each student. This activity is also effective when pitched instruments are substituted. Use Orff instruments or resonator bells, selecting pentatonic scale or chord tones.

Evaluation criteria: The student will play the instruments in the rhythm of a spoken chant. The chant will not be spoken aloud while playing, but the instruments will accurately reproduce the rhythm of the words. Each syllable should be articulated. The improvised parts should be added to the satisfaction of the teacher. The rhythm of the words of the chant should be accurately reproduced in two of three consecutive sessions.

SHORT-TERM OBJECTIVE C-4-i

Objective: The student will play a rhythm instrument in the rhythm of the words of a song (melodic rhythm).
The teacher will

- Select a song with a marked and uncomplicated melodic rhythm, such as "Chumbara," page 148.

- Ask students to keep time to the music in any manner that they wish—clapping, tapping feet, etc. Observe the students carefully; if one student is keeping time to the rhythm of the words, hand that student an instrument to play. Have the student stand where everyone can see and hear the rhythm being played. Ask all students to keep the same rhythm.

- Assign the same type of instrument (wood, metal, drum) to each student and ask the class to keep the rhythm demonstrated by the leader.

Equipment needed: One instrument of the same type for each student.
Evaluation criteria: The student will play a rhythm instrument, indicating each syllable of each word in a song. The rhythm will be played accurately in two of three consecutive sessions.

Chumbara

Canadian School Song

chum chum chum chum chum chum chum chum chum chum! Hi!

2. Fy-do-lee, fy-do-lee, fy-do-lee,
   fy-do-lee, fy-do-lee, fy-do-lee,
   fy fy fy fy fy fy fy fy! and repeated.

The exceptional student will play a rhythm instrument in the rhythm of the words of a song.

SHORT-TERM OBJECTIVE C-4-j

Objective: The student will play a rhythm instrument as an accompaniment to a song, indicating the pulse of the music.

The teacher will

- Select a song with a strong rhythmic appeal, such as "Stars and Stripes Forever," page 149.

- Sing the song or play a recording of the march; clearly indicate the steady underlying pulse of the music. This may be shown by foot tapping, hand clapping, or movement of the head or shoulders. A drum or other rhythm instrument may also be used. Ask students to keep time in the same manner.

- Identify a student who is keeping time accurately and ask that student to lead the class.

- Assign each student a rhythm instrument of one type (drum, wood, or metal), asking him to play his instrument in the same manner as the leader.

Equipment needed: One type of rhythm instrument; if possible, have one for each student.

Evaluation criteria: The student will accompany a song or a recording with a rhythm instrument, playing the pulse accurately in two of three consecutive sessions.

Stars and Stripes Forever

Words and music by John Philip Sousa

Hur - rah for the flag of the free,_____

May it wave as our stand-ard for-ev-er,

The gem of the land and the sea,

The ban-ner of the right!

Let ty-rants re-mem-ber the day

When our fa-thers, with might-y en-deav-or,

Pro-claimed as they marched to the fray, That by their

might, and by their right, It waves for-ev-er.

The exceptional student will play rhythm instruments, indicating the underlying pulse of the music.

Stodola Pumpa

Words by Rene Martin
Czech Folk Tune

Rather slowly

Walk-ing a-long, we sing a hap-py song,

All things are fine, we'll sing your song and mine;

Walk - ing a - long, we sing a hap - py song,

All things are fine, we'll sing your song and mine. Hey!

Much faster

Sto - do - la, sto - do - la, sto - do - la, pum - pa,

1. **2.**

Sto- do- la pum - pa, sto- do- la pum- pa, pum, pum, pum.

The exceptional student will play a rhythm instrument in the rhythm of the words, *only on the slow part.*

The exceptional student will play a rhythm instrument, indicating the pulse of the music, *only on the fast part.*

SHORT-TERM OBJECTIVE C-4-k

Objective: The student will play a rhythm instrument as an accompaniment to a song, indicating the accented first beat in each measure.

The teacher will

- Select a song with a well-marked accent on the first beat of each measure, such as "Yankee Doodle Boy," page 152.

- Sing the song, emphasizing the accented first beat of each measure by playing that beat on a large bass drum on a stand. (Use a lamb's-wool beater if possible and describe a large arc as the accent is played. Be sure that the drum is struck lightly so as not to drown out the singing.)

- Ask the students to observe how the drum is being played.

- Ask the students to imitate the action of the teacher in playing the drum as the song is sung again.

- Identify a student who is successfully imitating the teacher and ask that student to play the bass drum as the song is sung again.

- Repeat the procedure until all students have had an opportunity to play the drum.

Equipment needed: A large bass drum on a stand with a lamb's-wool beater is ideal; however, a small drum may be substituted.

Evaluation criteria: The student will play a rhythm instrument as accompaniment to a song, accurately indicating the accented first beat of each measure in two of three consecutive sessions.

Yankee Doodle Boy

Words and music by George M. Cohan

The exceptional student will play a rhythm instrument as an accompaniment to a song, indicating the accented first beat of each measure.

SHORT-TERM OBJECTIVE C-4-l

Objective: The student will play an ostinato on a melody instrument as an accompaniment to a song.

The teacher will

- Select a song in which one fragment may be used as an ostinato (repeated over and over through the song), such as F#–C# in the round "Hey, Ho! Nobody Home," page 153.

- Play the first two tones of the round on a xylophone-type instrument or the piano, repeating the tones several times in rhythm and chanting the words "Hey, ho!"

- Ask the students to chant the two words and move in some way to the rhythm of their chant. (When the chanting is established begin to sing the round, continuing to play the ostinato throughout.)

- Invite a student who is moving in rhythm to play the ostinato part.

- Repeat the process until all students have played the ostinato.

Equipment needed: At least one xylophone-type instrument, such as an Orff xylophone, metalophone, resonator bells, or bass bar bells. This type of instrument is useful because the tones to be used can be separated from the rest of the instrument. However, in the event such instruments are not available, a piano can be used. It may be necessary to mark the keys to be played with a piece of masking tape.

Evaluation criteria: The student will play an ostinato on a melody instrument as an accompaniment to a song; the rhythm and pitches will be accurately played in two of three consecutive sessions.

Hey, Ho! Nobody Home

Traditional English Round

The exceptional student will play an ostinato (F#–C#) on a melody instrument as an accompaniment to a song.

SHORT-TERM OBJECTIVE C-4-m

Objective: The student will play the roots of the chord on a melody instrument as an accompaniment to a song.

The teacher will

- Select a song with no more than two chords and with few chord changes, such as "La Cucaracha," page 155.

- Sing the refrain, asking the class to recall ways of showing the accented beat in each measure by some physical movement (swaying, swinging the arms, etc.).

- Ask students to show accented beat through physical movement.

- Ask students to stand and face the front of the room and turn to face the side of the room when they hear a different tone.

- Play:
    F F F C
    C C C F

- Play an introduction:
    F F F

    and then sing and play as follows:

    F   F
    La cu-ca-ra-cha, la cu-ca-ra-cha
    F   C
    Scur-ries up and scur-ries down!

    (Follow the same procedure for the remainder of the refrain.)

- Repeat the procedure, asking the students to show the accented beat in each measure as they listen and to turn as the song is sung again.

- Ask a student who is making the turns correctly and showing the accented beat to play the two tones. (Give necessary assistance, such as pointing to the correct tones on the instrument or pointing to the letter names:
    F F F C
    C C C F
    F F F C
    C C C F
    or using one color for F and a different one for C.)

Equipment needed: At least one xylophone-type instrument, preferably one having removable bars so that the two tones to be used can be removed from the instrument. However, a piano can be used. It may be necessary to mark the two tones with masking tape. This type of accompaniment will sound better when played on the lower-pitched instruments.

Evaluation criteria: The student will play the roots of the chord on a melody instrument as an accompaniment to a song. The rhythm and pitches will be accurate in two of three consecutive sessions.

La Cucaracha

Words by Florence Martin
Mexican Folk Tune

La cu - ca - ra - cha,   Home is an - y part of   town!

La cu - ca - ra - cha, la cu - ca - ra - cha,

Has his trou -bles and his woes! La cu-ca - ra - cha, la - cu -ca

ra - cha, Hunt -ed ev - 'ry where he goes!

        F   F   F   C7

2. Oh, the busy *cucaracha* Is a roving vagabond!
      C7   C7   C7   F
Going where he isn't wanted, Grabbing food of which he's fond.
      F   F   F   C7
He must always keep a moving, He can never stop to rest;
      C7   C7   C7   F
If he did, someone would catch him, He is nothing but a pest!

REFRAIN
           F   F   F   C7
La cucaracha, la cucaracha, Scurries up and scurries down!
          C7   C7   C7   F
*La cucaracha, la cucaracha,*Home is any part of town!
          F   F   F   C7
La cucaracha, la cucaracha, Has his troubles and his woes!
          C7   C7   C7   F
La cucaracha, la cucaracha, Hunted ev'ry where he goes!

The exceptional student will play the roots of the chord on a melody instrument as an accompaniment to a song.

NOTE: If a fuller accompaniment is desired, use all the tones of the chord:

$$\text{F} = \text{F A C}$$
$$\text{C}^7 = \text{C E G B}^\flat$$

SHORT-TERM OBJECTIVE C-4-n

Objective: The student will play short repeated melodic fragments as they occur in a song.

The teacher will

- Select a song with short repeated melodic fragments, such as "Pick a Bale of Cotton," page 157.

- Sing the song and pantomime playing the three tones—B C D— that make up the words "Oh Man-dy." (Pantomime playing a xylophone-type instrument in the air so that everyone can observe the left-to-right action. Hold a mallet and if possible use a visual representation of a keyboard instrument so that students will understand what is being pantomimed.)

- Sing the song again, asking students to pantomime playing the three tones.

- Sing the song again, playing the three tones on a xylophone-type instrument. (If possible, place the instrument where students can easily observe the tones being played.)

- Ask a student to play the three tones each time they occur in the song.

- Repeat the procedure until all students have played the repeated melodic fragment.

Equipment needed: At least one xylophone-type instrument, or a piano could be used. Orff instruments or resonator bells or bass bar bells are useful because the three tones to be used can be separated from the rest of the instrument, making it much easier to play.

Evaluation criteria: The student will play short repeated melodic fragments as they occur in a song. The fragments will be played in the proper place in the song and with accurate pitch and rhythm in two of three consecutive sessions.

Pick a Bale of Cotton

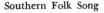

Southern Folk Song

You got to   jump down, turn a - round,   pick a   bale of cot - ton,

Jump, down,   turn a - round,   Pick a   bale a   day.

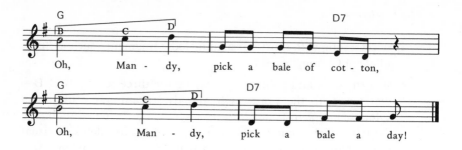

Oh,　Man - dy,　pick　a　bale　of　cot - ton,

Oh,　Man - dy,　pick　a　bale　a　day!

2. Oh, me and my partner can pick a bale of cotton
   Jump down, turn around, Pick a bale a day.
   B— C   D
   Oh, Man-dy, pick a bale of cotton,
   B— C   D
   Oh, Man-dy, pick a bale a day!

3. I went to Alabama To pick a bale of cotton,
   Jump down, turn around, Pick a bale a day.
   B— C   D
   Oh, Man-dy, pick a bale of cotton,
   B— C   D
   Oh, Man-dy, pick a bale a day!

The exceptional student will play short repeated melodic fragments as they occur in a song.

6 Moving

GOALS IN MOVING

Responding to music to the grestest possible extent by *moving* is a basic goal for all students, including the exceptional individual. Suggested annual goals which might derive from nondiscriminatory assessment of exceptional students:

D- 1. Will respond to music with any type of movement.
D- 2. Will respond to music by tapping feet.
D- 3. Will respond to the rhythm of music by swaying, bending, swinging, stretching.
D- 4. Will respond to the beat or pulse of music by walking.
D- 5. Will respond to the divided beat of music by running.
D- 6. Will respond to the rhythm of music by jumping.
D- 7. Will respond to the rhythm of music by hopping.
D- 8. Will respond to the rhythm of music by galloping.
D- 9. Will respond to the rhythm of music by skipping.
D-10. Will respond to the rhythm of music by performing in a group in a school assembly or community function.
D-11. Will respond to the rhythm of music by performing as a soloist in a school assembly or community function.

Goals in Moving

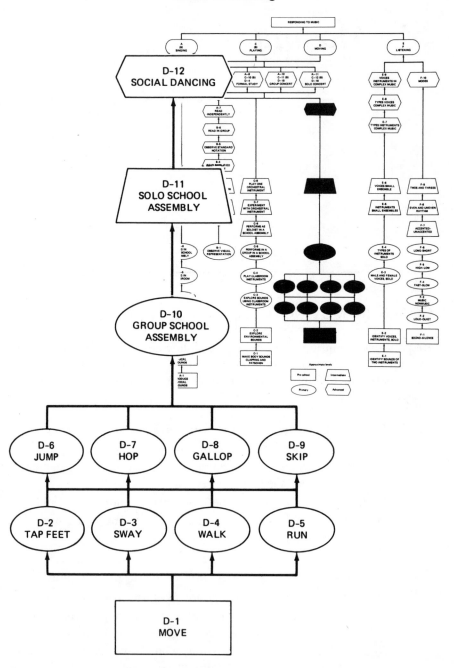

D-12. Will engage in social dancing.

D-13. Will engage in self-initiated dance activities.

D-14. Will engage in formal study of the dance.

D-15. Will perform in a dance group in a formal setting.

D-16. Will perform as soloist in a formal dance recital.

D-1 ANNUAL GOAL

The exceptional student will respond to music with any type of movement.

MASTERING THE ANNUAL GOAL

Mastery of this annual goal may be achieved through a variety of short-term objectives. Key ideas contributing to success include

Encouraging students' response by experimenting with many different types of music.

Praising students who respond.

Assisting students physically when necessary, but striving to make the students responsive to the music.

Modeling the required response when necessary, but striving to make the student responsive to the music.

SHORT-TERM OBJECTIVE D-1-a

Objective: The student will respond to a drumbeat with any type of movement.

The teacher will

- Place a large drum on a bare floor where there is plenty of space for students to move. (The large drum and bare floor will carry vibrations better than a covered floor and a small instrument.)

- Play a well-accented rhythm pattern repeatedly on the drum. A pattern such as

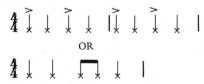

could be played.

- Urge students to move as the drum is heard. Urge them by example, pictures, words, and, if necessary, physical assistance.

Equipment needed: A large drum with a lamb's-wool beater is best; however, any resonant percussion instrument could be substituted.

Evaluation criteria: The student will respond to a repetitive rhythm pattern played on a drum with some type of movement during two of three consecutive sessions.

SHORT-TERM OBJECTIVE D-1-b

Objective: The student will respond to piano (or instrumental) music with any type of movement.

The teacher will

- Play music with a marked rhythm on the piano, the Autoharp, or the guitar (or use a recording of a popular piece).
- Urge the students to move as the music is heard. Urge them by example, pictures, words, and, if necessary, physical assistance.

Equipment needed: A source of music, preferably a piano; however, another instrument or a recording can be substituted.

Evaluation criteria: The student will respond to instrumental music with some type of movement in two of three consecutive sessions.

SHORT-TERM OBJECTIVE D-1-c

Objective: The student will respond to music, making at least one of the movements that are suggested in the words of a song.

The teacher will

- Sing a song that suggests movement, such as "I Can Move," page 163, moving as the words suggest.
- Urge the students to move.
- Substitute the name and movement of any student who is moving (see second verse).
- Ask students to move in the same manner as the student whose name was sung.
- Praise the students who respond.

Equipment needed: No special equipment is needed.

Evaluation criteria: The student will respond to a song by making some type of movement in two of three consecutive sessions.

I Can Move

Anon.

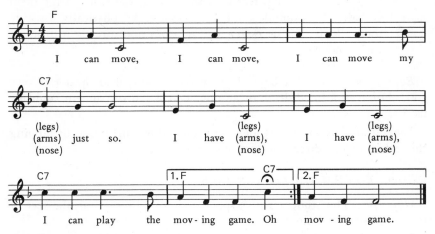

The exceptional student will respond to a song by making some type of movement.

D-2 ANNUAL GOAL

The exceptional student will respond to music by tapping the feet.

MASTERING THE ANNUAL GOAL

Mastery of this annual goal may be achieved through a variety of short-term objectives. Key ideas contributing to success include

Modeling the foot tapping with exaggerated action.
Reinforcing the beat by tapping.
Praising students who are responding.
Giving physical assistance where needed.

SHORT-TERM OBJECTIVE D-2-a

Objective: The student will respond to music by tapping the feet at the sound of a drum.

The teacher will

- Place a large drum on a bare floor and play a steady beat in a moderate tempo.

- Model tapping the feet with the drumbeat (exaggerating the movement).

- Urge students to tap feet with the beat of the drum. Urge them verbally, by example, and, if necessary, by physically assisting them. (It may be necessary to take a position directly in front of each student.)

Equipment needed: A large drum with a lamb's-wool beater is very good; however, a hand drum or another percussion instrument could be used.

Evaluation criteria: The student will respond to a drumbeat by tapping the feet in two of three consecutive sessions.

SHORT-TERM OBJECTIVE D-2-b

Objective: The student will respond to music by tapping the feet at the sound of the piano.

The teacher will

- Select a piece of music with a marked rhythm, such as "The Battle Hymn of the Republic," page 164.

- Play the piece on the piano (if a piano is not available, a recording can be substituted).

- Urge the students to tap their feet along with the music. Urge them verbally and by example, exaggerating the motion.

- Praise students who respond.

- Reward those who respond by asking them to be leaders.

Equipment needed: Music with a marked rhythm, preferably played on the piano; however, a recording can be substituted.

Evaluation criteria: The student will respond to music by tapping the feet at the sound of the piano during two of three consecutive sessions.

Battle Hymn of the Republic

Words by Julia Ward Howe
Early American Tune

Glo - ry, glo - ry, hal - le - lu - jah!

8va Low _ _ _ _ _

The exceptional student will respond to music by tapping the feet at the sound of the piano.

D-3 ANNUAL GOAL

The exceptional student will respond to the rhythm of music by swaying, bending, swinging, and stretching.

MASTERING THE ANNUAL GOAL

Mastery of this annual goal may be achieved through a variety of short-term objectives. Key ideas contributing to success include

Allowing ample space for free movement.

Encouraging students to make large arcs with their arms, shoulders, and upper torsos.

Encouraging students to sway in different directions.

Encouraging students to sway at different levels of height.

Encouraging students to sway in as many different ways as they can think of, always keeping their feet stationary.

SHORT-TERM OBJECTIVE D-3-a

Objective: The student will respond to the rhythm of music by swaying when given an aural and a visual cue.

The teacher will

- Show a picture of trees swaying in the wind. Focus attention on the fact that only the top of the tree moves. The tree does not move from one place to another.

- Ask students to imitate a tree being blown by the wind.

- Encourage students to stretch and sway, making a large arc with their arms, shoulders, and torsos.

- Praise students who are swaying naturally and freely.

- Identify one or two students who are responding as directed and ask them to take a piece of chalk in each hand, letting the chalk touch the chalkboard as they sway, producing a drawing such as:

- Play an accompaniment to the movement, either on the piano or on an Autoharp or a triangle. The accompaniment should be in $\frac{3}{4}$ meter with a strongly accented first beat—for example,

Use such piano music as "Skater's Waltz," page 167.

- Ask the class to sway with the students who are drawing the arcs.

- Encourage students to move freely and in different ways.

Equipment needed: A piano (or recording), a triangle, or an Autoharp.

Evaluation criteria: The student will respond to the rhythm of music by swaying when given an aural and visual cue. The student will respond appropriately in two of three consecutive sessions.

Skater's Waltz

E. Waldteufel

D-4 ANNUAL GOAL

The exceptional student will respond to the beat or pulse of music by walking, synchronizing steps and beat.

MASTERING THE ANNUAL GOAL

Mastery of this annual goal may be achieved through a variety of short-term objectives. Key ideas contributing to success include

Encouraging students to develop a free and easy walk, not a stylized imitation of someone.

Remembering that the walk is basic to social and folk dances.

Accommodating the speed of the beat (or tempo of the music) to the speed of the walkers, especially with beginners.

Identifying a large enough space so that students can move freely.

Encouraging students to walk in many different ways, thus nuturing creativity.

Praising effort rather than criticizing the end results.

Rewarding the student's ability to think in a creative (or different) way rather than commenting on the quality of response.

SHORT-TERM OBJECTIVE D-4-a

Objective: The student will respond to beat or pulse by walking in a natural and free manner accompanied by a drum.

The teacher will

- Identify a space large enough for each student to walk in a forward direction.
- Ask the students to walk forward (or toward an object in the room, such as the piano). Model the action if necessary.
- Listen to the sound of the student's footsteps and play a drum accompaniment that matches the speed of the majority of students.
- Encourage students to walk naturally and freely.
- Identify a student who is walking freely and with the drum and ask that student to lead the class.
- Reinforce the drum by saying, "Step, step, etc." or "Walk."

Equipment needed: A hand (or dance) drum and a lamb's-wool beater are ideal so that the teacher can move about the room; however, other kinds of percussion instruments (even hand clapping) can be used. Space is needed for this activity. If space is limited, work with one or two students at one time, having the other class members clap or play a percussion instrument.

Evaluation criteria: The student will walk in a free and natural manner when accompanied by a drumbeat during two of three consecutive sessions.

SHORT-TERM OBJECTIVE D-4-b

Objective: The student will respond to beat or pulse by walking backward to the accompaniment of a drum.

The teacher will

- Identify a space for walking.
- Ask students to walk forward to the accompaniment of the drum.
- Ask one or two students to retrace their steps without turning around (walk backward). (It will probably be necessary to model the activity and assist the students physically.)
- Remind the students to look over their shoulders so as not to hurt anyone.
- Give other students an opportunity to walk backward.
- Play an accompaniment (on the body of the drum) to the movement, reinforcing the beat by saying, "Step, step, etc." or "Walk."
- Ask students to walk forward or backward upon hearing drum signals:
  Drum—walk forward
  Body of drum—walk backward.

Equipment needed: A hand drum and a beater.

Evaluation criteria: The student will respond to the beat or pulse by walking backward to the accompaniment of the drum.

SHORT-TERM OBJECTIVE D-4-c

Objective: The student will respond to the beat or pulse of music by performing a simple pattern dance.

The teacher will

- Teach the students to sing a traditional singing game or a song such as "Step with Me," page 170.
- Be sure that the students are very familiar with the song. (If the words indicate the motions, be sure that students understand the words.)
- Select about eight students to form a circle.
- Take a place in the circle so as to model the responses.

- On the words "Step and step and step with me, It's as easy as can be," walk in a circle. On the words "Step, step in," step toward the middle of the circle. On the words "step, step out," step backward to the original position. On the words "Then you turn yourself about," turn around in place.

Equipment needed: No special equipment needed.

Evaluation criteria: The student will respond to the beat or pulse of music by performing a simple pattern dance (or singing game) during two of three consecutive sessions.

Step With Me

German Folk Tune

The exceptional student will respond to the rhythm of music by performing a simple pattern dance.

SHORT-TERM OBJECTIVE D-4-c

Objective: The student will respond to the beat or pulse of music by walking in an individual and creative manner.

The teacher will

- Encourage students to walk at different levels of height by asking such questions as, "Can you walk as though you are trying to paint the ceiling?" or "Can you walk as though you were only the size of a cat?"

- Encourage students to walk at different speeds by asking such questions as, "Can you walk as though you are in a hurry?" or "Can you walk as though it is a beautiful day and you don't want to go in?"

- Encourage students to imitate animals, story characters, etc. by asking such a question as, "How does a lion walk?" or "How does a robot walk?"

- As students improvise their walking, play a drum (or piano) in their rhythm.
- Select a piece of music such as "Leo the Lion," page 171, without telling the students the title, encouraging them to walk in whatever way the music suggests.

Equipment needed: A drum or piano to accompany the students' movement, and a piece of rather descriptive music (the music should be suitable for walking, usually in $\frac{4}{4}$ or $\frac{2}{4}$ meter). This activity requires plenty of space.

Evaluation criteria: The student will respond to the beat or pulse of music in some individual and creative manner in two of three consecutive sessions synchronizing steps and beat.

Leo the Lion

Vic Marantz

The exceptional student will respond to the rhythm of music in an individual and creative manner.

SHORT-TERM OBJECTIVE D-4-d

Objective: The student will respond to the rhythm of music by swaying upon hearing music in $\frac{3}{4}$ meter (waltz) and walking upon hearing music in $\frac{2}{4}$ meter (march). Movement and steps will be synchronized to the meter and beat.

The teacher will

- Review what is meant by swaying to music.

- Play music in $\frac{3}{4}$ meter, such as "Skater's Waltz," page 167, or play a three-beat pattern on the triangle:

- Ask students to sway to the music, encouraging them to think of other ways to sway by asking such questions as, "How would you sway if you were pushing someone in a swing?" (front to back) or ". . . in a very low swing?" (near the ground) or ". . . in a very high swing?" or ". . . a very light person?" or ". . . a very heavy person?"
- Review ways in which students can walk to music (different levels, different size steps, etc.; see D-4-c Objective).
- Ask students to walk to the music of the piano, recording, or drum.
- Explain that students will hear two different kinds of music, some suitable for swaying and some for walking. Ask students to listen carefully and walk or sway according to the signal that the music gives.
- Play music in twos and threes intermittently, either on the triangle and drum, as

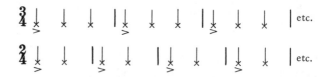

or on the piano, using music such as "Music for Swaying and Walking," page 173.

Equipment needed: A piano is preferable; however, percussion instruments such as a drum and triangle can be substituted. A recording can also be used.

Evaluation criteria: The student will respond to the meter and beat of music by swaying upon hearing music in $\frac{3}{4}$ meter and walking when hearing music in $\frac{2}{4}$ meter. The student will respond accurately in two of three consecutive sessions.

Music for Swaying and Walking

Adapted from "One Man Went To Mow"

D-5 ANNUAL GOAL

The exceptional student will respond to the divided beat in music by running, synchronizing steps and beat.

MASTERING THE ANNUAL GOAL

Mastery of this annual goal may be achieved through a variety of short-term objectives. Key ideas contributing to success include

> *Providing* ample space so that students can run freely and safely.
> *Insisting* that students start and stop running on signal, in order to maintain control.
> *Urging* students always to listen to the accompaniment.
> *Reminding* students to watch where they are going and to heed rules of safety.

SHORT-TERM OBJECTIVE D-5-a

Objective: The student will respond to the divided beat by running to the accompaniment of a drum, starting and stopping with the drumbeat.
The teacher will

- Identify a large area in which students will be asked to run.

- Make students aware of the necessity of following directions to start and stop on signal from the drum, and the necessity of watching so that they do not bump into one another.

- Demonstrate running, starting and stopping with the drumbeat and staying within the allowed space.

- Play a light, quick beat on the rim of the drum, explaining that it is the signal for running.

- Ask one or two students to demonstrate running, starting and stopping with the drumbeat and staying within the allowed space.

- Ask others to run, praising those who stay within the allowed space and start and stop with the drumbeat.

- Encourage students to run lightly and naturally, playing a moderate running tempo.

Equipment needed: A hand drum (and beater) is preferable; however, any percussion instrument can establish the beat, even hand clapping or finger snapping.

Evaluation criteria: The student will respond to the divided beat by running to the accompaniment of a drumbeat. The student will start and stop with the drum and run within the allowed space in two of three consecutive sessions.

SHORT-TERM OBJECTIVE D-5-b

Objective: The student will respond to the beat or divided beat by running or walking on the appropriate drum signal.

The teacher will

- Identify the space that is available.

- Review the drum signal for walking, and ask students to walk to the drumbeat.

- Review the drum signal for running, and ask the students to run (play a faster drumbeat on the rim of the drum and the slower walking signal on the head to make it easier for students to differentiate between the two).

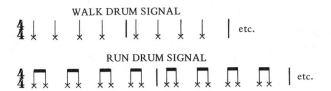

- Ask students to follow the drum signals, interspersing walk and run signals. (Be sure to include periods of silence as well, so that students will have periods of rest.)

Equipment needed: A hand (dance) drum with a lamb's-wool or felt beater.

Evaluation criteria: The student will respond to the beat or divided beat by running or walking on signal from a drum, responding appropriately in two of three consecutive sessions.

SHORT-TERM OBJECTIVE D-5-c

Objective: The student will respond to the beat and divided beat in music by running when eighth notes occur and walking when quarter notes occur in short passages of music. Steps will be synchronized with beat and divided beat.

The teacher will

- Identify the space that is available for the activity.
- Play piano music (or a recording) at a comfortable walking tempo, asking the students to walk in a large circle, all moving in the same direction.
- Play piano music at a comfortable running tempo, asking the students to run in a large circle, all moving in the same direction. (It is usually necessary to remind students to use all of the space, since they tend to crowd together.)
- Give the students many opportunities to both walk and run accompanied by the piano music, insisting that they start and stop with the music.
- Explain that the students will now hear some music that signals running and some that signals walking, and that they are to follow the piano signals. (See "Music for Running and Walking," page 176).
- Explain that students are to hold their position ("freeze") when the piano stops, making the activity like a game.

Equipment needed: A piano is preferable; however, a recording can be substituted.

Evaluation criteria: The student will respond to the beat and divided beat in music by running, walking, or stopping on signal from the piano. Steps will be synchronized with the beat and divided beat in two of three consecutive sessions.

Music for Running and Walking

Traditional English Singing Game
Adapted

Run, Run etc.

Repeat ad lib.

The exceptional student will respond to the beat and divided beat in music by running, walking, or stopping on signal from the piano.

D-6 ANNUAL GOAL

The exceptional student will respond to the rhythm of music by jumping, synchronizing movement and music.

MASTERING THE ANNUAL GOAL

Mastery of this annual goal may be achieved through a variety of short-term objectives. Key ideas contributing to success include

> *Providing* plenty of space so that students can jump freely and safely.
> *Encouraging* students to jump with a spring and land on the balls of their feet with bent knees.
> *Encouraging* students to find many different ways to jump.

SHORT-TERM OBJECTIVE D-6-a

Objective: The student will respond to the music by jumping as indicated in the words of a song.

The teacher will

- Select a song in which the words indicate a jumping motion, such as "The Clapping Land" (second verse), page 178.
- Teach the students to sing the first stanza of the song very well.
- Sing the second stanza and ask for a volunteer to show the class the activity required by the words (jumping).
- Identify ample space for each student to jump freely and safely.
- Sing the song, asking all students to jump appropriately.

- Help students discover that if they keep their heads and shoulders up, bend their knees to start, use their arms and legs to start, and then land on the balls of their feet, they can spring higher.

- Encourage students to jump in many different ways by asking such questions as, "Can you jump higher?," ". . . faster?," ". . . slower?," "Can you bounce?"

- Sing the song several times, asking the students to find different ways of jumping.

Equipment needed: No special equipment is needed; however, ample space is required to ensure safety and freedom.

Evaluation criteria: The student will jump as indicated by the words of a song in two of three consecutive sessions.

The Clapping Land

Words adapted by Hase Regen
Danish Folk Song

2. When I was trav'ling o'er the sea,
    I met a man who said to me,
    "If you would sail the great North Sea,
    Then jump and jump and jump with me.

Jump and jump and jump with me, come with me, come with me,
Jumping Land is where you'll be,
Far across the great North Sea."

The exceptional student will respond to the rhythm of the music by jumping as indicated in the words of a song.

SHORT-TERM OBJECTIVE D-6-b

Objective: The student will respond to accent by jumping to the accompaniment of a drumbeat.

The teacher will

- Identify a large space and see that students are spread around the area in order to jump freely and safely.

- Encourage students to jump in as many ways as possible, modeling as necessary.

- Observe the students' rate of jumping and adapt a drumbeat to their jumping. Encourage students to listen to the drum and jump with the drum. Reinforce the beat by saying, "Jump, jump, etc."

- Vary the tempo and dynamics by playing slower, faster, getting faster, getting slower, softly, loudly, getting louder, getting softer, etc. Play the drum in a rhythm such as

or play the piano music such as "Music for Jumping," page 180.

- Encourage students to plan and implement a sequence of movements that they know, such as

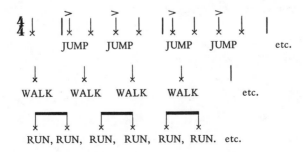

- Play an accompaniment to the combination of movements chosen by the students and have the class engage in the activity.

Equipment needed: A piano or a drum.

Evaluation criteria: The students will jump by standing with both feet on the floor, elevating themselves and landing on both feet. They will land on the balls of their feet and with slightly bent knees. This activity will be synchronized to the rhythm of the piano or drum in two of three consecutive sessions.

Music for Jumping

American Folk Melody
Adapted

The exceptional student will respond to the rhythm of music by jumping to the accompaniment of the piano or drum.

D-7 ANNUAL GOAL

The exceptional student will respond to the rhythm of music by hopping, synchronizing movement and music.

MASTERING THE ANNUAL GOAL

Mastery of this annual goal may be achieved through a variety of short-term objectives. Key ideas contributing to success include

Providing plenty of space so that students can hop freely and safely.

Encouraging creativity by suggesting imitation of frogs, rabbits, balls, machines, etc.

Urging students to spring and land on the ball of one foot.

SHORT-TERM OBJECTIVE D-7-a

Objective: The student will respond to the rhythm of music by hopping on one foot.

The teacher will

- Demonstrate hopping and ask students to recall where they have seen anyone hopping (hopscotch).
- Remind the students that hopping is on only one foot and that it is important to land on the ball of the foot with bent knee— as in jumping.
- Ask a few students to demonstrate the hop.
- Identify space for hopping and ask all students to hop.
- Ask one or two students to think of a shape (square, circle, etc.) and hop on the floor in that shape. Have other students guess the shape they have chosen to hop.
- As the students hop, adapt an accompaniment to the rhythm of the hop, playing a piano or tone block.

Equipment needed: A piano or tone block.

Evaluation criteria: The student will hop by putting weight on one foot, elevating himself and landing on the same foot, accompanied by piano music or a tone block. The student will be successful in two of three consecutive sessions.

SHORT-TERM OBJECTIVE D-7-b

Objective: The student will respond to the rhythm of music by combining hopping and walking.

The teacher will

- Identify ample space for students to hop without bumping into one another.
- Ask the students to hop freely about the room.
- Ask students to rest as needed.

- Demonstrate combining hopping and walking, saying, "Hop and hop and hop and hop and walk, walk, walk." Play a rhythm on the tone block, such as

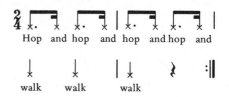

- Ask students to hop and walk as indicated by the rhythm and the words.

- Ask students to listen to the first four measures of "Music for Hopping," page 182, to identify places where the music suggests hopping and other places where it suggests walking.

- Ask students to respond as the music suggests.

- Identify a student who is responding to the dotted rhythm by hopping and the steady rhythm by walking and ask that student to lead the class.

Equipment needed: A tone block and if possible a piano or a recording.

Evaluation criteria: The student will respond to a dotted (uneven) rhythm by hopping and to a steady (even) beat by walking.

The student will respond appropriately in two of three consecutive sessions.

Music for Hopping

German Folk Tune
Adapted

The exceptional student will respond to the rhythm of music by combining hopping and walking.

SHORT-TERM OBJECTIVE D-7-c

Objective: The student will respond to music by hopping, synchronizing the hops with the music.

The teacher will

- Identify ample space for students to hop without bumping into one another.
- Ask students to hop about the room, accommodating an accompaniment to the hopping.
- Ask students to hop more slowly, and accommodate an accompaniment to their tempo.
- Ask students to listen to the accompaniment and adjust their hopping to the accompaniment.

Equipment needed: A piano, Autoharp, guitar, or drum.

Evaluation criteria: The student will hop by putting weight on one foot, elevating himself and landing on the same foot, synchronizing the hopping with the music in two of three consecutive sessions.

D-8 ANNUAL GOAL

The exceptional student will respond to the rhythm of music by galloping, synchronizing movement and music.

MASTERING THE ANNUAL GOAL

Mastery of this annual goal may be achieved through a variety of short-term objectives. Key ideas contributing to success include

> *Encouraging* students to gallop freely, using all available space.
> *Encouraging* students to imitate big horses, teams of horses, ponies, etc.
> *Urging* students to gallop in different ways—slow, fast, at different height levels, etc.

SHORT-TERM OBJECTIVE D-8-a

Objective: The student will respond to the rhythm of music by galloping to the accompaniment of a drum.

The teacher will

- Have the students sit (preferably on the floor) in a large room which has a hard-surfaced floor.
- Recall some of the rhythmic activities that the students have mastered (walking, jumping, hopping, running, etc.).
- Ask two or three students to demonstrate at least three of these activities.
- Ask the class to close their eyes as the three students demonstrate an activity and listen to the sound of feet to determine which activity the three students are demonstrating.
- Ask the class to close their eyes again and demonstrate the gallop.
- Ask the class to clap the sound of the feet. (Repeat as needed.)
- Model the gallop as students observe.
- Ask a few students to try to gallop.
- Ask entire group to gallop in a large circle, moving in the same direction.
- Experiment with starting the gallop on either foot.
- Adapt an accompaniment to the students' galloping rhythm. (Use

a drum or play the piano. See "Music for Galloping or Skipping,"
page 185.)
Drum rhythm:

Equipment needed: A drum or a piano.

Evaluation criteria: The student will gallop to the accompaniment of
the piano or drum in two of three consecutive sessions.

Music for Galloping and Skipping

Flemish Folk Tune

The exceptional student will respond to music by galloping.

SHORT-TERM OBJECTIVE D-8-b

Objective: The student will respond to the tempo or speed of music
by changing the speed of his or her galloping as the accompaniment
changes, synchronizing movement and music.

The teacher will

- Identify a space large enough in which students can move freely
  around the room without bumping into one another.
- Play the uneven rhythm of the gallop on the drum or the piano.
  See "Music for Galloping or Skipping," page 185. Ask the students
  to listen to the speed of the gallop rhythm.

- Ask students to gallop at the speed of the accompaniment.
- Vary the tempo, playing slower, faster, getting slower, getting faster, etc., asking the students to follow the speed of the accompaniment.

Equipment needed: The piano or a drum.

Evaluation criteria: The student will respond to the rhythm of the music by changing the speed of his or her gallop as the accompaniment changes. The student will synchronize movement and music in two of three consecutive sessions.

D-9 ANNUAL GOAL

The exceptional student will respond to music by skipping, synchronizing movement and music.

MASTERING THE ANNUAL GOAL

Mastery of this annual goal may be achieved through a variety of short-term objectives. Key ideas contributing to success include

> *Encouraging* students to skip in a free and natural manner.
> *Providing* plenty of space.
> *Urging* students to skip at many different levels (high, low, medium), at different speeds (faster, slower, getting faster, getting slower), and with different amounts of force (heavy, light, strong, weak).

SHORT-TERM OBJECTIVE D-9-a

Objective: The student will respond to music by skipping to an accompaniment.

The teacher will

- Identify a large space where students may skip safely and freely.
- Model skipping, asking the students to observe, saying, "Skip-ping, skip-ping, skip-ping. . . ."
- Ask students to skip in a line led by the teacher, continuing to chant.
- Find a student who skips well to lead the line.
- Observe students and identify those having difficulty.

- Ask all students to walk slowly, rather than skip, saying, "Walk, walk, walk, walk. . . ."
- Repeat the procedure until the rhythm of the walk is well established; then change the chant to, "Walk, hop, walk, hop, walk, hop. . . ."
- Demonstrate pulling first one knee up and then the other.
- Give students many opportunities to skip, making positive comments so as to help students respond freely.
- Add an accompaniment when the skipping is established. Play a percussion instrument or the piano. See "Music for Galloping and Skipping," page 185.
- Vary the speed of the accompaniment, urging the students to vary the speed of their skipping as the accompaniment changes.

Equipment needed: A piano or a percussion instrument for an accompaniment. A recording may be substituted if necessary.

Evaluation criteria: The student will respond to music by skipping to an accompaniment.

SHORT-TERM OBJECTIVE D-9-b

Objective: The student will respond to music by skipping when an uneven beat is heard and walking when an even beat is heard, synchronizing movement and music.

The teacher will

- Identify ample space for free rhythmic activity.
- Review skipping by chanting, "Skip-ping, skip-ping" and clapping the long–short beats as the class skips.
- Play a drum or piano accompaniment to the skipping. See "Music for Galloping and Skipping," page 185.
- Teach a song that combines two rhythmic responses, such as skipping and walking, is found in "Rig-jig-jig," page 188.
- Ask students to listen to the song to determine which part has even beats.
- Divide the class and ask one group to clap the part of the song having the even beat and the other group to clap the part having the uneven beats.

- Ask students to identify the music that is suitable for skipping and the one suitable for walking. (It may be necessary to chant the words "Walk, walk, walk" and "Skip-ping, skip-ping" as a reminder.)
- Sing the song, asking the students who clapped the uneven rhythm to skip and the group who clapped the even beats to walk.
- Alternate groups.
- Play the music (or sing the song), asking students to respond to the entire song, skipping or walking as indicated by the music.

Equipment needed: No special equipment is needed; however, a piano would be useful.

Evaluation criteria: The student will respond to the music by walking when an even beat is heard and skipping when an uneven beat is heard. The student will perform accurately in two of three consecutive sessions, synchronizing movement and music.

Rig-Jig-Jig

Traditional American Song

The exceptional student will respond to the rhythm of music by walking when an even rhythm is heard and skipping when an uneven rhythm is heard.

REFERENCES

ABESON, A., and J. ZETTLE. "The End of the Quiet Revolution: The Education for All Handicapped Children Act of 1975." *Exceptional Children* 44 (2 Oct. 1977): pp. 114–28.

BEER, A., and M. HOFFMAN. *Teaching Music What, How, Why.* Morristown, N.J.: General Learning Press, 1973.

BEH Data Notes. Washington, D.C.: Bureau of Education for the Handicapped, U.S. Department of Health, Education, and Welfare, Sept., 1977.

BIRGE, E. B. *History of Public School Music in the United States.* Bryn Mawr, Pa.: Oliver Ditson Company. Theodore Presser Co., 1937.

BIRKENSHAW, L. *Music for Fun, Music for Learning.* Toronto: Holt, Rinehart and Winston of Canada, Limited, 1974.

BRUCE, W. "The Parent's Role from an Educator's Point of View." In *The Hearing Impaired Child in the Regular Classroom,* edited by W. H. Northcott. Washington, D.C.: A. G. Bell Association for the Deaf, 1973.

CAREY, M. A. *Music for the Educable Mentally Handicapped.* Dissertation Abstracts, Vol. 19, 2967, University of Michigan, Ann Arbor, 1958.

DOREN, G. A. "The Status of the Work-Ohio." *Proceedings of the Association of Medical Officers of American Institutions for Idiotic and Feebleminded Persons.* Session: June 8–12, 1878 (in Syracuse, N.Y.). Philadelphia: J. B. Lippincott and Co., 1879, pp. 103–4.

EAGLE, C. *The Music Therapy Index.* Vol. 1. Lawrence, Kansas: The National Association for Music Therapy, Inc., 1976.

GEARHEART, B. and M. WEISHAHN. *The Handicapped Child in the Regular Classroom.* St. Louis: C. V. Mosby Company, 1976.

GELINEAU, R. P. *Songs in Action.* New York: McGraw-Hill Book Company, 1974.

GRAHAM, R. M., comp. *Music for the Exceptional Child.* Reston, Va.: Music Educators National Conference, 1975.

——— *Music for the Young Atypical Child.* Reston, Va.: The Council for Exceptional Children, 1977.

JENKINS, E. *The Ella Jenkins Song Book for Children.* New York: Oak Publications, 1972.

KIRK, S. A. "Comments on the Carey Research." In *Mental Retardation,* edited by H. A. Stegens, and R. Heber. Chicago: University of Chicago Press, 1964.

LEVIN, G., H. LEVIN, and N. SAFER. *Learning Through Music.* Boston: Teaching Resources Corporation, 1975.

MOVETON, E. F. "Report of the Special Class Department: Cleveland, Ohio." *Proceedings of the Journal of Psycho-Asthenics.* American Association for the Feebleminded, 1904–1905.

National Advisory Committee on the Handicapped, 1976 Annual Report. *The Unfinished Revolution: Education for the Handicapped.* Washington, D.C.:

U.S. Department of Health, Education, and Welfare, 1976. U.S. Government Printing Office stock number 017-080-01532-3.

NORDOFF, P., and C. ROBBINS. *Music Therapy in Special Education*. New York: Harper & Row Publishers, Inc., 1971.

"Official Actions of the Delegate Assembly." *Exceptional Children* 43 (Sept. 1976): p. 43.

ORFF, C., and G. KEETMAN. *Music for Children*. New York: Schott Music Corp. (Associated Music Publishers, Inc.), 1956.

PRICE, D. E. "Music for Every Child (Except 53.3%)." *Music Educators Journal* 39 (June 1953): p. 25.

Public Law 94-142, The Education for All Handicapped Children Act of 1975. Washington, D.C.: The United States Congress, 1975.

REYNOLDS, M., and J. W. BIRCH. *Teaching Exceptional Children in All America's Schools*. Reston, Va.: The Council for Exceptional Children, 1977.

ROBBINS, CLIVE, and P. NORDOFF. *First Book of Children's Play Songs*. Bryn Mawr, Pa.: Theodore Presser Company, 1962.

——— *Fun for Four Drums*. Bryn Mawr, Pa.: Theodore Presser Company, 1968.

——— *Spirituals for Children*. Bryn Mawr, Pa.: Theodore Presser Company, 1972.

——— *Songs for Children with Resonator Bells and Piano*. Bryn Mawr, Pa.: Theodore Presser Company, 1973.

SPILMAN, B. W. "Religious Freedom for the Feebleminded." *Journal of Psycho-Asthenics* 49. Edited by H. W. Potter. American Association for the Feebleminded, 1925: p. 251.

STEINBACH, C. "Report of the Special Class Department: Cleveland, Ohio." *Proceedings of the Journal of Psycho-Asthenics* reprinted in American Journal of Mental Deficiency, 1904–1905. Phila & La., 1905, p. 106.

TORRES, SCOTTIE. *A Primer on Individualized Education Programs for Handicapped Children*. Reston, Va.: The Council for Exceptional Children, 1977.

TREGOLD, A. F. *Mental Deficiency*. London: Bolliere, Tindall and Cox, 1922.

WALSH, G. *Sing Your Way to Better Speech*. New York: Dutton & Co., Inc., 1947.

WILBUR, C. T. "Classroom of a School Year at the Illinois Asylum for Feeble-Minded Children." *Proceedings of the Association of Medical Officers of American Institutions for Idiotic and Feebleminded Persons*. Sessions: October 3, 1828. Reprinted with the permission of The American Association on Mental Deficiency, Inc., by Johnson Reprint Corp., 111 Fifth Avenue, New York, N.Y. 10003.

Index